Mastering Your iPhone

11

iPhone 11 User Guide for Beginners, New iPhone 11 Users and Seniors

Tech Reviewer

TABLE OF CONTENT

How to Use this Book

Welcome! Thank you for purchasing this book and trusting us to lead you right in operating your iPhone 11 device on iOS 13. This book has an updated list of all the current tips and tricks available for the latest software upgrade in the Apple family.

To better understand how the book is structured, I will advise you first read from page to page, after which you can then navigate to particular sections as well as refer to a topic individually. This book has been written in the simplest form to ensure that every user understands and gets the best out of this book. You can also use the well-outlined table of content to find specific topics faster and more efficiently.

Introduction

In 2018, Apple launched the iPhone XR alongside the iPhone XS and XS Max. The XR was the most affordable amongst the trio. This made it famous among users and several people considered it the best iPhone ever introduced by the Apple family. Now, Apple has introduced the iPhone 11 to replace the iPhone XR, and seeing that Apple did not go with the alphabet names for their new releases shows us where the Apple company has positioned these new devices. The dual-camera setup, satisfying speed boost, and longer battery life has even given the iPhone 11 a higher edge over the iPhone XR from last year. Let's not also forget the low price, which has made it the best iPhone for most people.

Camera Improvements

One outstanding physical feature of the new iPhone 11 is the 12-megapixel dual camera. You will think that Apple designed these new iPhone releases to make the camera bump eye-catching intentionally. You can barely notice the single camera on the iPhone XR, while the dual-camera bump design on the XS will not ordinarily make you think twice about what it will look like. But the dual camera on the iPhone 11 snatches your attention in a way that says, "Smile! You're on camera!"

While the iPhone 11 comes with the wide and ultra-wide cameras, the iPhone XR has only a single wide camera. The ultra-wide camera of the iPhone 11 offers a 2x zoom out option, which allows you to capture more of whatever is in the environment you are shooting. The ultra-wide camera gives you more flexibility when capturing pictures. Thankfully, it is also easy for you to switch between the ultra-wide and the wide camera mode. When shooting in the camera app, you will see a 1x button at the bottom of the image frame to notify you that you are on the wide camera mode. Click on this button to switch to the ultra-wide mode, and then the 1x will change to 0.5x. Click on this same button again to return to the wide camera mode. Also, when shooting in the 1x camera view, you will see a preview of what it will be like to shoot with 0.5x ultra-wide mode.

Looking from the picture quality for both camera modes, you are sure to produce great-looking photos on the wide and ultra-wide modes. The colors are sharp, and the cameras give this stunning level of image clarity and details. Although this has always applied to other recent iPhone models, one thing though is the new Night mode that is exclusive to the iPhone 11 and iPhone 11 Pro. Night mode converts images you shot in dark environments and with the help of software processing, brings out details that you will not ordinarily see. You will see a guide on how to use the night mode later in this book.

Shooting on Night Mode

One issue with the rear camera on the iPhone 11 is the absence of the optical zoom, which was also missing in the iPhone XR. The iPhone 11 gives only digital zoom, up to 5x. In some cases, mostly when going above the 2x digital zoom, you begin to get noticeable image noise, which makes the photo look unsightly. So, if you love to use the zoom feature very often, you may need to check how you use it on this particular iPhone. It is worthy of mentioning that Apple upgraded the front-facing TrueDepth camera to a 12-megapixel camera that shoots 4K/60fps video camera from a 7-megapixel camera that shoots 1080p/60fps video. You can now use the front camera to record slow-motion videos, which Apple calls the "slofies."

Liquid Retina HD Display

Another feature that did not change in the iPhone 11 is the display. The iPhone still maintains the 6.1-inch LCD screen while the Pro has an OLED display. Apple refers to the iPhone 11 screen as a "Liquid Retina HD," and it has 625 nits of brightness, Retina display of 326 PPI resolution, and a 1,400 to 1 contrast ratio. When you place the iPhone 11 series beside each other, you will have to look hard to see the difference in their front display. The iPhone 11 Pro has a brighter screen, sharper details, and deeper colors. But without any comparison, the screen of the iPhone 11 looks great. The color brightness, quality and sharpness are also great. The OLEDs, of course, are higher than the LCD, but the LCD has its good quality, and except you need to get the best, the iPhone 11 will suit all your needs.

Faster Processor

While the iPhone XR operated on the A12 Bionic processor, the iPhone 11 witnessed an upgrade to A13 Bionic. The iPhone 11 performs faster than the iPhone XR. With A13, iPhone 11 has a 14% increase in terms of single-core CPU performance while it experienced an 18% increase in multi-core CPU performance. Apps in the new iPhone launch faster while graphics performance when playing games is smoother. The iPhone 11 Pro has the same feature with the iPhone 11, and so for fewer dollars, you get the same performance in your iPhone 11 that is in the iPhone 11 Pro.

Battery Life

Apple confirmed that the 3,046 mAh battery of the iPhone 11 would last one hour more than the iPhone XR that had a 2,942 mAh battery. This battery life gives you up to 10 hours of streaming videos, 17 hours of video playback, and 65 hours of audio playback. Apple no longer provides an estimate for Talk time. According to a representative from Apple, the company achieved a longer battery life by combining a bigger battery with hardware and software optimization. You will not need to charge your iPhone all through the day as a test on active use, left the iPhone battery at 24 percent at the end of the day, without charge.

The only issue is the charger included in the phone box. The box comes with a 5-watt slow charger. But you can get the 18W USB-C power adapter for $29, the type that is in the 11 Pro and Pro Max. The iPhone also supports the wireless charge, but you need to get the Qi wireless charger separately.

iPhone 11 Design

When it comes to industrial design, the iPhone 11 still looks like the iPhone XR with the display notch, anodized aluminum sides, and the glass back available in green, Product Red, black, yellow, white, and purple. The colors for the iPhone 11 are not as bright as those of the XR. The iPhone 11 has the black bezels that are thicker than the OLEDs iPhones. The thicker bezels are used in LCD phones to stop light leakage. The other noticeable change in the design of the iPhone 11 from the XR, apart from the camera bump and colors, is the placement of the Apple logo. The logo is now placed in the center rather than near the camera. The Apple logo helps users to know where to place their devices for wireless charging.

Water-Resistant

Another commendable change is the improvement in water resistance from 1 meter to 2 meters for up to 30 minutes. Your phone can stay in water up to 2meters deep without fear of damage. The iPhone 11 does not also feel like a cheaper version of the 11 Pro models. It is comfortable to use, solid, and feels good when held.

Price

The price of the iPhone 11 is another feature that endears it to users. The 64GB model goes for $699, which is $50 lesser than the amount the iPhone XR was launched at while the iPhone 11 Pro goes at an introductory price of $999 for its 64GB version and the Pro Max goes for $1,099 for the same version.

For those with the iPhone 8 or older that have always desired to upgrade, this may be time to take action. You will get a longer battery life as well as a great improvement in speed. You will also enjoy the night mode feature, as well as the dual camera of the iPhone 11. However, you will need to be familiar with the no home button and the move from Touch ID to Face ID, but this will only take you some days to get used to.

iOS 13 on the iPhone 11

All the trio iPhone 11 has the new iOS software that comes with several features, which we shall highlight below.

Features of the iOS 13

Improvement to FaceTime

With iOS 13, we see some FaceTime video calls improvement, particularly positioning the eye while on calls. FaceTime in iOS 13 will use ARKit to scan your face and softly modify the position of your eyes to make it seem as if you are directly looking into the eyes of your caller rather than at the screen.

HomeKit

HomeKit also has its additions. Apart from the small changes to the UI, we have the addition of the HomeKit secure video. Some security cameras that are HomeKit-enabled will now be stored to the HomeKit on a deeper level. This update will allow you to save your video recordings in iCloud as well as be able to control the exact time to record footage.

Routers are not left out as Apple aims to give some security controls and privacy to routers. Apple announced that routers are now supported in HomeKit, and you can use the Home app to control the services and devices that can communicate with your router. Not all routers will support this feature, though.

Airplay 2 speakers, too, have more controls. You can now use the Airplay 2 speakers to play radio stations, playlists, and specific songs through scenes and automatons.

Dark Mode

Every iOS 13 devices have a dark mode feature. Dark mode places a dark background and highlights on the phone's iOS and all the Apple default apps like messages, emails, and so on. Apple has also encouraged developers to install this feature on third-party apps. You can permanently enable this mode or you can modify it to come on at a particular time or period. In the later part of this book, you will see how to achieve this.

Messages

The Message app also witnessed an upgrade. You can now automatically share your profile picture and name with people when you begin a conversation with them. You can set this option to apply to everyone or just with selected people. This guide will show you how to enable the feature. It is now also straightforward to search through messages. Click on the search bar in the messaging app, and you will see recent messages, photos, people and other options. As you type, the results get refined.

Privacy

Apple has always taken the privacy of its users seriously, and we also saw this in iOS 13. Thanks to the new granular controls, you can now control the apps that can access your location data. When you launch an app, you can choose to give the app access to your location only once or for each time you use the app. Apps will no longer be able to access your location through Bluetooth and Wi-fi. You also have greater control over the location data on your photos. When you share your pictures, you can choose whether you want the receiver to be able to view the location of the photograph or not.

Accessibility

I can say that the most significant accessibility change that we see in iOS 13 is the voice control addition, which makes it easy for you to control your phone with your voice. The system uses the Siri speech recognition algorithm to confirm that your input is correct while allowing users to include custom words. Personal data is also secure and safe as the phone leverages device processing.

Find My

The **Find My Friend** and **Find My iPhone** features were combined into one app in iOS 13, called the **Find My** app. This app allows you to discover your devices marked as lost even if they are offline.

Siri

Siri can now read out incoming messages using Airpods, and you can give an instant response. This function will work without the wake word and is also available with third-party messaging apps that have the Sirikit inbuilt. You also have the ***Share Audio Experience*** that allows you to share music with your friends through the Airpods quickly. For the HomePod, once you get back home, Siri will stop playing music when you tap your phone.

Siri now has access to 100,000 radio stations all over the world through the Live radio feature and it also has a sleep timer feature.

Lastly, you can use the Suggested Automations located in the Siri shortcuts to create your routines.

Photos and Cameras

We now have a new lighting effect with the portrait camera mode called the **High Key Mono**. You can also change the intensity of the light using the editing features, which will make the skin to appear smooth and brighten the eyes. This is similar to the moving lights found in a studio. The image editing feature available in the photo's app has a swipe-based control as well as a new design. Now, most settings you use for stills can also be used to edit your videos. You can now rotate videos as well as add filters. The photo library will delete duplicate photos while it concentrates on what Apple considers your best shots. It then organizes the photos into months, days, or years, and you can see them in a new album view.

Live videos and photos will now autoplay in the tab for new images, and you can also see the event, location or holiday, etc. in that same tab. The photo tab also has a new birthday mode that gives you access to view the photos of people on their birthday.

All your screen recording will now be grouped into a single place so that you do not have to go far to find them.

Animoji and Memoji

The Animojis and Memojis have more customization options including glasses, makeup, jewelry as well as changing the look of your teeth. Your character can also make use of Airpods. You can access default Memoji stickers through your device keyboard that you can share across apps like WeChat, Messages, and Mails.

Sign in with Apple

This feature is an easy and fast way to sign in to services and apps without having to input your social media login details. The feature authenticates your sign-ins using your Apple ID while ensuring that your details remain hidden. This new service uses the TouchID and FaceID as well as a 2-factor authentication system. For apps that require you to verify via email, Apple will generate a random email address linked to your primary email to keep your real details private.

Apple Maps

The Apple maps experienced several alterations and additions, including the addition of beaches, roads, buildings, along with heightened details. The map also has a new feature for favorites on your main screen, as well as a collection menu to help you organize your favorites and planned trips. There is also the introduction of the **Look Around,** which is similar to Google's **Streetview,** to give you a view of a location before you visit.

In this guide, you will learn how to use each feature for the map. Other additions include being able to share your ETA with your family and friends, get updated flight information, real-time updates on public transportation as well as an improved Siri navigation.

Reminders

Reminders now have the toolbar to add in times, dates, and attachments. Also, there has been a significant improvement with the message app integration to allow both apps to communicate together. This update means that you can set a reminder about someone, and the reminder will pop up when next you message the person.

Siri is now integrated with the reminders app. You can type longer words while Siri will provide related suggestions to what you are typing. Siri is also programmed to read out reminders, so, when chatting in the Message app, Siri reminds you of things it assumes you should remember.

Health App

All the functions that are on the new WatchOS health app are now available on the iPhone, like the menstrual cycle tracking and the activity trends. The main app also has a new summary view to display notifications and a highlight section where you will see your health and fitness data over time. The app uses machine learning to show things that are of utmost importance to you. It is either encrypted securely on iCloud or stored on your phone, and you can decide to share any of the details with other people

Getting Started: Unboxing the iPhone 11

What is in the Box

- The iPhone device
- 18W USB-C Power Adapter
- EarPods with lightning connector
- A limited user guide

Setting up your iPhone 11

You can set up your new iPhone 11 in various ways, whether you want to start anew, restore apps from another phone or import data and content from a phone that is not an Apple device. First, let me explain what these options mean for iPhone 11 users.

Option 1: Starting anew means beginning the setting from scratch, and this applies to people who have not used a smartphone before or a phone with internet services.

Option 2: You can import data from your old device that is not an Apple brand, like Windows, Android, or Blackberry, using the Apple app in

Google play, particularly for Android users. This option is suitable if you are moving to the iPhone from your android.

Steps to Setup the iPhone 11

- The first step is to power on your new device by pressing and holding the side button. Once the screen comes up, you will see the "Hello" greeting in various languages.

- Next, a slider will show on the screen with a ***Slide to Set Up*** option, click on this option.
- Choose your Language, Region, and Country. You must select the right information as this will affect how information like date and time etc. will be presented on the device.
- Now, you have to connect your device to a cellular or Wi-Fi network to activate your phone and continue with the setup. You should have inserted the SIM card before turning on the phone if going with the cellular network option. To connect to a Wi-Fi network, tap the name of your Wi-fi, and it connects automatically if there is no password on the Wi-fi. If there is a security lock on the Wi-fi, the screen will prompt you for the password before it connects.
- Next, is to manually set up your iPhone 11 by tapping "**Set up Manually**." You can

choose the **"Quick Start"** option if you own another iOS 11 or later device, then follow the onscreen instruction. Proceed with the manual setup if you do not have any other iOS devices.

- To set up manually, read the Data and Privacy Information from Apple and then click on "**Continue.**"
- Click on ***"Enable Location Services"*** to grant access to apps like **Maps** and **Find my Friends.** You can turn off this option whenever you want. You will see how to turn on the location services and how to turn it off in a later part of this book. You can also click on "***Skip Location Services***" if you wish not to set this feature yet.
- The next step is to set up Face ID. You will need the Face ID to unlock your device as well as to authenticate your purchases.
- To set up the Face ID at this stage, click on **Continue** and follow the instructions you

see on your screen. You can also do this step later by clicking on "**Set Up Later in Settings.**" Please refer to the instructions on how to set up Face ID in a later part of this book.

- The next step is to register alternate faces. You can either add another appearance of yourself or add a friend or family member as an alternate face. Setting an alternate face can be helpful for times when the device is unable to recognize you because of a change in appearance. To do this, go to Settings, click on **"Appearances"** and then click on ***"Set Up an Alternative Appearance"*** to complete the registration
- Whether you register the Face ID now or not, you will need to create a personal four digits code to protect your device. With this passcode, you will be able to access Face ID and Apple Pay. Tap **"Passcode Option"** if you will rather set up a

four-digit passcode, custom passcode, or even no passcode.

- With an existing iTunes or iCloud backup or even an Android device, you can move your backed-up data to the new device or move contents from the old to the latest smartphone. If you wish to restore via iCloud, select “**Restore from iCloud Backup”** or select “**Restore from iTunes Backup”** for restoring from iTunes. However, if this is your first smartphone, select “**Set Up as New iPhone.”**

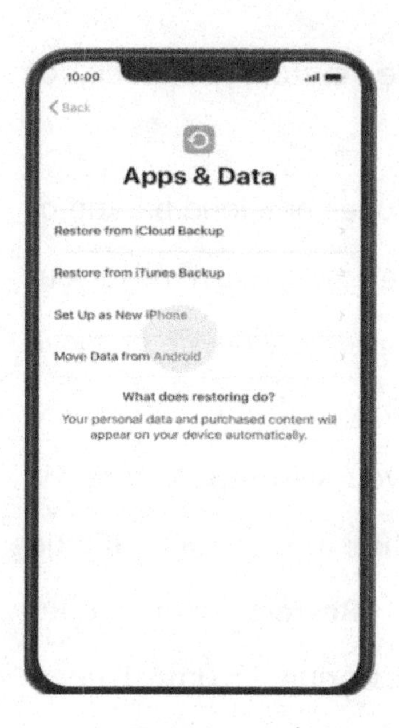

- To proceed, you need to input your Apple ID. For those with an existing Apple account, put in your ID and password to sign in. If you don't have an Apple ID or maybe you have forgotten your login details, click on **"Don't have an Apple ID or forget it."** If you have more than one Apple ID, you should choose the option **"Use different Apple IDs for iCloud & iTunes."**

- On the next screen, accept the iOS terms and conditions to move on.
- The next step is to set up Siri and other services you will need on your device. You need to train Siri to recognize your voice by speaking a few words to Siri.
- You can also choose to set up the iCloud keychain and Apple Pay at this point.
- Also, set up screen time to inform you of how much time you spend on your device

and then set a time limit for the length of time you make use of apps.

- Turn on automatic update and other needed features
- Now click on "**Get Started**" to finish this startup and begin to enjoy and explore your new smartphone.

SIM Card Slot

Apple finally put in a dual SIM feature in the iPhone 11, meaning you can have two registered lines actively working on one phone. You will need a double SIM to set up your iPhone 11.

- Use a SIM eject tool or a paper clip to insert in the small hole housing the SIM tray.
- Pull out the SIM tray.
- Check for the notch located in the corner of your SIM card.
- Place the SIM face down at the bottom of the card Tray, ensure it matches as you will be unable to close it if it doesn't match.
- Place the second SIM in the tray at the top.
- Once done, push the SIM holder back to its correct position, and your SIM is ready for use.

Turning on iPhone 11

The following steps will show how to turn on the iPhone 11:

- Press the **Side** button until the iPhone comes on.

- Once you see the Apple logo, release the button and allow your iPhone to reboot for about 30 seconds.
- Once the iPhone is up, you will be required to input your password if you have one.

Turning off iPhone 11

Follow the steps below to turn off your iPhone 11:

- Hold both the volume down and the side button at the same time.
- Release the buttons once you see the power off slider.
- Move the slider to the right for the phone to go off.
- You may also use the side and volume up button, the only thing is, you may take a screenshot in error rather than shut down the phone.

Going Home on your iPhone 11

- Regardless of where you are on your iPhone 11, to return to the home screen, swipe the screen from the bottom up.

Apple ID

- Go to the **Settings** option.
- At the top of your screen, click on **Sign in to your iPhone.**
- Choose **Don't have an Apple ID or forgot it?**
- A pop-up will appear on the screen, and you click on **Create Apple ID**.
- Input your date of birth and click on **Next.**
- Then input your first name and last name then click on **Next.**
- The next screen will present you with the email address option. Click on **"Use your current email address"** if you want to use an existing email or click on **"Get a free**

iCloud email address" if you want to create a new email.

- If using an existing email address, click on it and input your email address and password.
- If creating a new one, click on the option and put your preferred email and password.
- Verify the new password.
- The next option is to select 3 Security Questions from the list and provide answers.
- You have to agree to the device's Terms and conditions to proceed.
- Select either **Merge** or **Don't Merge** to sync the data saved on iCloud from reminders, Safari, calendars, and contacts.
- Click on **OK** to confirm the **Find My iPhone is turned on.**

Launching Apple Pay

- Click on the side button twice to begin the Apple Pay process when you want to make a payment in the app store.

Apple Pay Setup

Before you can use Apple Pay, you need to ensure that your device is on the latest iOS version. Then add your card, either debit, credit, or prepaid cards to your iPhone. You should be signed in to iCloud using your Apple ID. If you want to use the Apple Pay account on more than one device, you need to add your card to each of the devices. The steps below will guide you on how to add your cards to Apple Pay:

- Go to Wallet and click on ⊕
- Follow the instructions on the screen to add a new card. On iPhone 11, you can add as much as 12 cards. You may be required to add cards linked to your iTunes, cards you have active on other devices, or cards

that you removed recently. Chose the cards that fall into the requested categories and then input the security code for each of these cards. You may also need to download an app from your card issuer or bank to be able to add your card to the wallet.

- When you select **Next,** the information you inputted will go through your bank or card issuer to verify and confirm if the card can work on Apple Pay. Your bank will contact you if they need further information before completing the verification.
- After the card is verified, click **Next** to begin using Apple Pay.

Checking out with Apple Pay

Here are useful steps to check out on Apple Pay for your daily transactions:

- Once you are ready to make your payments at a checkout terminal, double-press the side button to open the Apple Pay screen.
- Look at the iPhone screen to verify with Face ID (or enter your passcode).
- Then place the iPhone 11 near the payment terminal.
- If you're using Apple Pay Cash, double-press the side button to approve the payment.

Unlock Your Device

- From the home screen, swipe up to unlock your device or to return to the home screen when in an app.

Get the Home Button Back

If you were using iPhone 8 or 7 previously, you might have a hard time operating the iPhone 11 without a home button. Thankfully, you can use a software home button to replace the physical home button with the steps below:

- Go to the settings app.
- Click on **General**
- Then tab **Accessibility.**
- Select **Assistive Touch** and set your preferred shortcuts for double tap, 3D Touch, single tap and long press for the Assistive Touch button.
- You can choose the Single tap option to serve as your home button while you set up other options to access any other feature of choice.

New QuickTake Feature

To begin shooting a video, just press and hold the shutter button, as you do with Snapchat. The video will maintain the same frame but will capture as a photo, which is quite impressive. To record the video for a longer time, swipe right on the shutter to get it locked into video recording mode.

Choose Ringtone

- From the Home screen, go to **Settings.**
- Click on **Sounds & Haptics.**
- Then click on **Ringtone.**
- You may click on each of the ringtones to play to help you choose the most suitable.
- Select the one you like then click the "**< Back**" key at the top left of the screen.
- Slide the page from the bottom up to return to the Home screen.

Choose Message Tone

- From the Home screen, go to **Settings.**
- Click on **Sounds & Haptics.**
- Then click on "**Text Tone.**"
- You may click on each of the message tones to play so you can choose the one you prefer.

- Select the one you like then click the "**< Back**" key at the top left of the screen.
- Slide the page from the bottom up to return to the Home screen.

Set/ Change Language

- From the Home screen, click on the **Settings** option.
- Select "**General**" on the next screen.
- Then click on **Language and Region.**
- Click on **iPhone Language** to give you options of available languages.
- Choose your language from the drop-down list and tap **Done**.
- You will see a pop-up on the device screen to confirm your choice. Click on **Change to (Selected Language),** and you are done!

Set/ Change Date/ Time

- From the Home screen, click on the **Settings** option.
- Select "**General**" on the next screen.

- Then click on **Date & Time.**
- On the next screen, beside the "**Set Automatically"** option, move the switch to the right to turn it on.
- Slide the page from the bottom up to return to the Home screen.

Notification Bar

From the notch of your phone, swipe down to go to the notification center.

Access Control Center

- From the right top side of your screen, swipe down to launch the control center.

Customize the Control Center

You can quickly access those features you often use from the control center without having to launch the Settings app. However, you will need to customize this feature as the default setting does not consider this. Follow the steps below

- Go to the control center.

- Click on **Customize Controls.**
- You will see the default shortcuts to include a **timer, flashlight, camera, and a calculator**. You can add more shortcuts like the Notes app, alarm, and others.

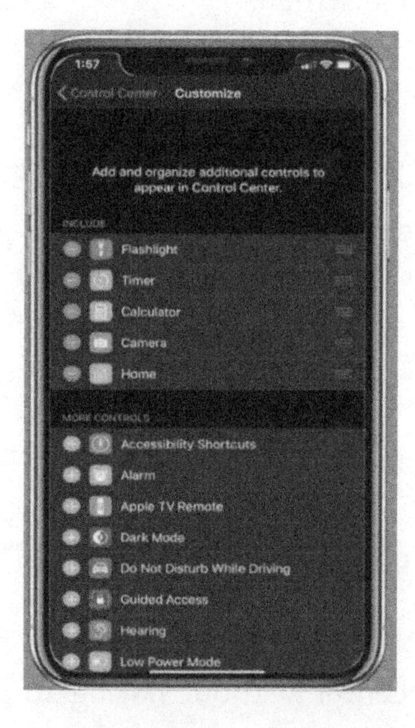

How to Use the Control Centre

- From the right side of the notch, swipe down to view the control center.
- Click on the needed function to either access it or turn it on or off.

- Move your finger up on the needed function to choose the required settings.
- Once done, return to the home screen.

Control Centre Settings

- Go to **Settings> Control Centre.**
- On the next screen, beside the '**Access within Apps'** option, move the switch to turn it on or off.
- Click on **Customize Controls.**
- For each function you want to remove, click on the minus (-) sign.
- To add icon under **More Controls,** click on the plus (+) sign at the left of each of the icons you want to add.
- Click on the move icon beside each function and drag the function to the desired position in the control center.
- And you are done.

Connect to Paired Bluetooth Devices from Control Center

As is usual, clicking on the Bluetooth button will either enable or disable Bluetooth. Now iOS 13 has added the 3D Touch feature to display devices and also connect. With this new addition, you do not need to exit a current app to look for the settings app and all the long processes available in the other versions. Should you need to pair a device to Bluetooth, you can now do so from the control center without exiting the current app you are on. The steps are below:

- Launch the control center. Swipe from the right top side of the iPhone down to the access control center.
- You can either 3D touch or click and hold the wireless connections block at the top right side of the screen to expand it.

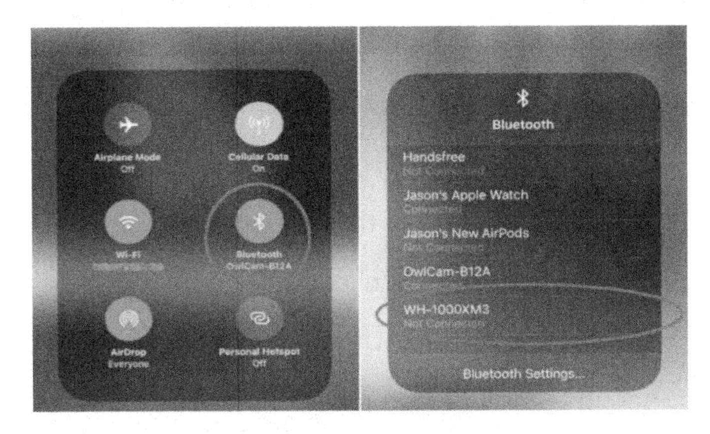

- 3D Touch or Tap and hold the Bluetooth button on the right side of the screen.
- You will see a list of all paired Bluetooth devices, whether connected or not.
- Select the one you wish to connect to, and you are fine.

Connect to Wi-Fi Through the Control Center

Most of us join new Wi-fi networks very frequently, whether at a friend's place, a restaurant, or while on a flight. iOS 13 has now made it easier to connect. Rather than launching the settings app to be able to view the Wi-fi menu, you can now connect directly from the control center. Again, you will not need to exit an app to do this. See the steps below.

- Launch the control center. Swipe from the right top side of the iPhone down to access the control center.
- You can either 3D touch or click and hold the wireless connections block at the top right side of the screen to expand it.
- 3D Touch or Tap and hold the Wi-Fi button on the left side of your screen.

- You will see a list of all paired nearby Wi-fi networks, whether connected or not.
- Select the one you wish to connect to, and you are fine.

Cycle Tracking

The health app in the Apple device is a great tool, and iOS 13 has brought more additions, the biggest of this addition is the cycle tracking. With this tool, you can track your menstrual cycle and also have tools to alert you when you are at your most fertile days, and when you are due. To get started, follow the steps below

- Launch the health app.
- Then choose **Search**, and click on **Cycle tracking** from the displayed list.
- Click on **Get started**, then click on **Next.**
- The app will ask you a series of questions like the duration of your period and the date the last one started.
- You will also get options on ways you will like to track your period; you can also choose to receive notifications and predictions on when you are likely to see the next cycle. You will also select whether you will like to record spotting

and symptoms in your cycle log and whether you want to be able to view your fertility Windows.

- As soon as you have provided all the answers, you will return to the homepage for **Cycle Tracking.**
- On this screen, click on **Add Period** to add your previous menstrual cycle days.
- You can also click on **Spotting, Symptoms,** and **Flow Levels** option to input more specific details.

True Tone Display

True Tone could be helpful as it automatically modifies the white balance of your phone's display to reflect changes in light conditions. It is enabled by default on your phone. However, you can decide to disable it if you do not fancy the idea.

- Go to the settings app.
- Then click on **Display and Brightness.**

- Navigate to **True Tone** and move the switch to the left to disable the feature.
- You can always follow the steps above to enable the feature when desired.

Tap to Wake

While the **Tap to Wake** feature can be beneficial, it can also be activated accidentally. You can disable it with the steps below:

- Go to the settings app.
- Click on **General**
- Then tab **Accessibility.**

- Navigate to **"Tap to Wake"** and move the button to the left to disable.

Attention Awareness

With the Face ID system, the Apple software can determine whether you are staring into your phone or not. Because of this, it can perform several functions like dimming your phone screen when you are not staring into it or even placing the phone on silence automatically. You can disable this feature with the steps below:

- Go to settings.
- Click on **Face ID and Passcode.**
- Navigate to **Attention Aware Features** and move the switch to the left to disable the feature.

Sign-IN-With-Apple

It can be quite tiring having to log in each time you launch a different app, and at the same time, you may not be comfortable signing in with your Instagram account to all apps. The Sign-in with Apple feature allows you to quickly sign into apps using your Apple account without sharing personal information.

- For apps that support this feature, you will see the option displayed on the opening screen of the apps.
- Click on it, and you will receive a prompt to log in to your Apple account.
- Then you will select the information you desire to share with the app developer.
- With this feature, you can decide to share your email address or not to share it.
- If you do not want to share your email address, Apple will generate a random email address that will automatically forward messages to your Apple iCloud email address while keeping your anonymity safe.

The Apple Map

Favorites in the Apple Maps

I know that the Apple map has been available for some time now, but not so many like using it. The good news is that the iPhone 11 has an improved Apple map that includes more beaches, roads, building and other details that may interest you. Apart from these listed ones, some other cool features were just added, like being able to add a location to your list of Favorites. You can also arrange the saved locations in your personally customized collections. Follow the steps below to add a favorite on the map.

- Search for a location or tap on a location.
- Scroll down to the bottom and click on **Add to Favorites.**
- You can always access your favorites list on your main page.

To add a particular location to your customized collection,

- Drag up from the Apple maps on the main page.
- Then click on **My Places.**
- Select **Add a Place.**
- On the next screen, you can now add any location that you recently viewed to your collection or search through your search bar for the location.

To begin a new collection,

- Navigate back to your apple maps on the main page.
- Swipe from the bottom of the screen upwards.
- Then click on **New Collections** to make a new list.

Look Around Feature

Look around is Apple's version of the **Streetview** from Google, as it allows you to preview a location before you visit. Follow the steps below on how to use it.

- Type in a location on your Apple maps.
- Then select it by pressing long on the map.
- If the location supports **Look Around,** you will find a **look around** image on that location.
- Click on it to move down to Street level and drag to navigate around.
- While on this view, you can also see facts about the place or even add it to your favorites list by swiping up from the bottom of the screen.

Customize Your Memoji and Animoji

To do this,

- Go to iMessage.
- Tap on a conversation to launch it.
- Click on the Memoji icon, then tap the "+" button.

Save Your Passwords

Similar to iOS 12, you can have your logins and passwords saved to your iCloud keychain. Whenever you log in to a service, the system will ask if you will like to save your login details to the iCloud keychain. However, you can now manually manage your details. To do this,

- Go to **Settings.**
- Click on ***Passwords & Accounts***.
- Then select ***Website & App Passwords.***
- You may receive a prompt to use your passcode, Face ID, or Touch ID to access this screen.

Play Live Radio Through Siri

Although this feature was available in iOS 12, however, iOS 13 brought about some new additions. This function is quite easy. You can just say to Siri, "Hey Siri, "play [name of radio station] radio station." As long as Siri has access to the requested radio station, it will begin to play the station. Siri works with various online radio providers to bring you your desired radio station.

Add Siri Shortcuts

This function lets you assign quick actions to your virtual assistant, Siri. While this feature came with iOS 12, however, the iPhone 11 has a more pronounced function for Siri, and you also have the Siri shortcut app on its own in the iPhone 11 device.

- To get started, click on the **Siri shortcut app** to launch it
- Then click on **Create Shortcuts** to create a simple type of shortcut.
- With the **automation** tab, your device can intelligently react to context as they change. For instance, you can customize the shortcut to play a particular song each time you get home or design the button to

automatically send your location to your partner whenever you are heading home from work.

- In the **Gallery** function, you will find a range of predefined shortcuts to give you some inspiration in designing yours, or you can even make use of the predefined shortcuts.

Screen Time

For those who have used other iPhone devices on iOS 12 before, you may be familiar with this feature. But in case you are not, it's quite simple to set up, and it will help you to know how much time you spend on your iPhone. To begin with screen time,

- Go to **Settings**
- Then click on **Screen time.**

Set App Limits

If you really want to watch your usage, you can set a duration on time spent in using a particular app with the App Limits feature available under Screen Time. The steps below will guide you on how to do it.

- Go to **Settings**
- Then click on **Screen time.**
- Select **App Limits.**
- Then click on **Add Limit.**
- Now, the new addition in iOS 13 allows you to choose apps that belong to the same category and then group them to have the same app limit. This means that you can limit your usage of Spotify, Twitter, and Fortnite to a combined total of 6 hours every day.
- Once you hit the limit, you will get a splash screen, notifying you that limit has breached as well as give you the option to

ignore the deadline for the remainder of the day or just for 15 minutes only.

Backup Using iCloud

This step is probably the simplest way to back up your device

- Connect your device to a Wi-Fi network.
- Go to the settings app.

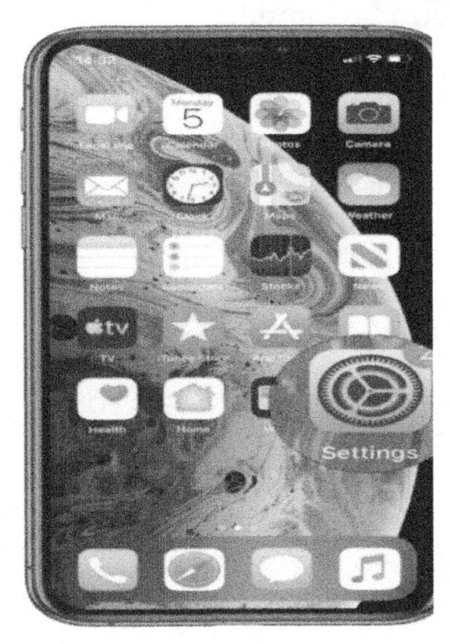

- Click on your name at the top of the screen.
- Then click on **iCloud**.

- Navigate down and click on **iCloud backup**.
- Then select **Back Up Now.**

To be sure that the phone backed up, follow the steps below

- Go to settings.
- Click on **iCloud.**
- Then select **iCloud Storage.**
- And choose **Manage Storage** on the next screen.
- Then click on your device from the list.

Back Up with iTunes on PC or Mac

if you have a Windows PC or an older Mac, you can use the iTunes to back up your iPhone with the steps below:

- Confirm that the iTunes is updated to the latest version then connect your iPhone.
- Follow the instructions on the screen and enter your passcode if requested or activate the ***Trust This Computer*** option.

- In the iTunes app, click on your iPhone.
- Then click on ***Back Up Now*** to back up your device.

Take a Screenshot

Screenshots help you to note down problems you wish to seek help for later. Without the home button, taking a snapshot may seem tricky; however, follow these steps to help you make the best shots possible.

- Press both the Volume Up and the side button simultaneously to take a screenshot of the page.
- The photo from the screenshot will be saved automatically in the Photos app, under the **Screenshots** album.
- To edit the photo, go to the picture and tap the thumbnail at the left bottom corner of your iPhone.

Take a Slofie

To take a Slofie, set the camera to use the front-facing camera then swipe to get to the new slo-mo function to begin using the front-facing camera to make slow-motion videos or Slofie, as Apple calls it.

Offload Unused Apps

You can set your device to uninstall apps that you have not used for a long time. When the app is uninstalled, it will still retain the app data on your phone.

- From the **Settings,** go to **iTunes and App Store.**
- At the bottom of the screen, besides **"Offload Unused Apps,"** move the switch left or right to activate or disable the function.

App Switching

Switching Apps can be tricky without a home button, but the below steps will make it as seamless as possible.

- To open the App Switcher, swipe up from the bottom of the screen and then wait for a second.
- Release your finger once the app thumbnails appear.
- To flip through the open apps, swipe either to the left or to the right, and select the app you want.

Force Close Apps

You do this mostly when an app isn't responding.

- Merely swiping up from the bottom of the screen will show the app switcher. This will display all the open apps in a card-like view.
- Locate the app from the app switcher and swipe up to close the app.

- Tap on the minus button for each of the apps you wish to close.
- To go through apps used in the past, swipe horizontally at the bottom of your home screen.

Home Screen Icons

The steps below show how to arrange the home screen icon on your iPhone 11.

- Press and hold any icon until all the icons begin to wiggle.
- Drag the icons into your desired position.
- Tap either the **Done** button at the right upper side of the screen or swipe up to exit the wiggle mode.

'Find My' App

In iOS 13 interface on iPhone 11 series, Apple combined the **Find My iPhone** and **Find My Friends** feature into an app they called **Find My.**

With this feature, you can share your location with your loved ones and friends as well as find your devices on the same app. It is simple to use with the steps below

- Go to your home page and launch the **Find My** app.
- Under the **People** tab, you will see your current location.
- Click on the **Start Sharing Location** tab to share it with your contact.
- Type in your desired contact to share with.

To find your missing device,

- Click on the **Device** tab to modify your map to present all the registered Apple devices on your account.
- Click on the missing device then select from any of the options on the screen: ***Mark As Lost*, Get Directions** to the device, **remotely *Erase This Device,*** or ***Play Sound.***
- If any of the devices is currently offline, you can set the map to alert you once the

device is connected to the internet. Click the ***Notify Me*** option.

Reminders app

The iPhone 11 series have an improved Reminders app thanks to the introduction of iOS 13. When you launch the reminders app, you can view the total reminders you have at the moment with the ones that are due today. To add a new task to the list,

- Click on **All.**
- Then click the "+" button located underneath each category to add a new task

You can also add a reminder time or date, change the category for a task, or set to receive a reminder of a task in a specified location by clicking on the blue **'i'** icon once you have tapped on the desired tasks to launch the options.

Create a Reminder

- Launch the reminders app.
- Then click on **reminders** under **My List** heading.
- Then select **New Reminders** at the bottom of your screen, on the left side.
- Fill in your details for the reminder.
- Then click **Return** on your keyboard to confirm your first reminder.

Add Location, Time or a Connected person

It's one thing to add a reminder, and it's another thing to have to go through your to-do list for reminders of what you intend to do in the day. Now you can add a time or location to your reminder so that your phone can prod you at the right time or place. After you have set your reminder, click on the blue **"i"** icon that is located on the right side of your task to access the task options.

- To be reminded at a specific time, enable the option to ***Remind me on a day*** and then fill in details in the option for ***Alarm or Reminds me at a time.***
- For recurring tasks, you can set the option to repeat.
- To add location, you should go for the option of ***Remind me at a*** **location** and then select your desired location.
- If your task has to do with someone, then you can set the reminder to alert you about the task whenever you message the contact. To do this, click on ***Remind me when messaging*** and then choose your preferred contact.

Get Siri to Remind You

With your virtual assistant, you do not always have to launch the reminders app and begin inputting details to remember an event or activity. You can say to Siri, "remind me to," followed by the contents of what you will like to be reminded of. You can also ask Siri to remind you at a specific place or time.

Add SubTasks

For complex projects or tasks, you can add sub-tasks, or you can even create a multi-entry list for your shopping. If you have a reminder that needs to have the subtasks set,

- Go to the task from your reminder app.
- Click on the blue **"i"** icon to launch the options.
- Then navigate down on your screen to the option for **Subtasks.**
- Click on it and then tap **Add Reminder** to include a subtask.
- Feel free to add as many subtasks as you like.
- Once done, you will find your subtask under the Reminder or the main task.

- You can complete the subtasks separately from the parent task.
- You can also click on the **"i"** icon to add its own time, separate location, or contacts for each subtask.

Today Notification Feature

You may have noticed that the reminders app has a new home page, which is self-explanatory. However, there is one important feature that is not revealed. By default, the reminders app will notify you of the tasks you have for each day. But you can change when you want the notification to happen or if you're going to want to receive any notification. To effect this change,

- Go to the settings app.
- Click on **Reminders.**
- On the next screen, you can completely turn off notifications or change the timing of the option of **Today Notification.**

- On this same screen, you can modify your tasks' default list.

Create a List

This new modifications in the reminder app can get us carried away with filling every little detail from tax notifications, to birthdays to grabbing milk on your way from work. The good thing is that you can organize your tasks into lists to declutter your reminders home page. The steps below will show you how to create a list.

- Launch the reminders app
- Then click on the **Add list** found at the right bottom of the screen.
- Select from the varieties of logos and colors to help you tell the different lists at a glance.
- Once satisfied with your list, click on **Done** at the right top side of your screen.
- To add reminders or tasks to the list, click on the list from under the ***My Lists***

subheading and create them or move existing tasks to the list

- For an existing task, open the task, then click on the **"i"** icon to access the options.
- Go down and click on **List** then choose from your new list.

Note: if you are not able to quickly find a task, use the search bar option in the reminders app to search for the task.

Add a List to a Group

Now you have created a list and moved tasks to the list. However, there is more. You can add lists in the same categories to a general group. So, for instance, you have a list containing anniversaries and another one containing birthdays, you can group both of them into an 'important date' group to keep your home page looking appealing.

Follow the easy steps below to create your group

- Go to the homepage for the Reminders app.
- At the right top corner of your screen, click on **Edit.**
- Then click on **Add Group** at the bottom left of your screen.
- Input your preferred group name and choose all the lists you want to add to the group.
- Then tap **Done.**
- To modify the lists in each group, click on **Edit** again.
- Then click on the **"i"** icon next to the group.
- Then remove or add lists using the ***Include*** option.

How to Customize Today View

Today View feature houses various shortcuts and widgets that are useful like your weather forecast, calendar, and even the Siri app recommendations. You can access it on the home screen when you swipe left. However, you will only enjoy this feature if you customize it to suit your personal needs. The steps below will show you how to modify what you see on the Today view.

- Swipe left on the home screen to go to **Today View.**
- Navigate to the bottom of your screen and click on **Edit.**
- The next screen will show you all the apps downloaded on your phone with widgets that you can include in the Today View.
- Click on the ones you will like to add.
- You can also rearrange the widgets, drag the bars to the edge of your screen, on the right.

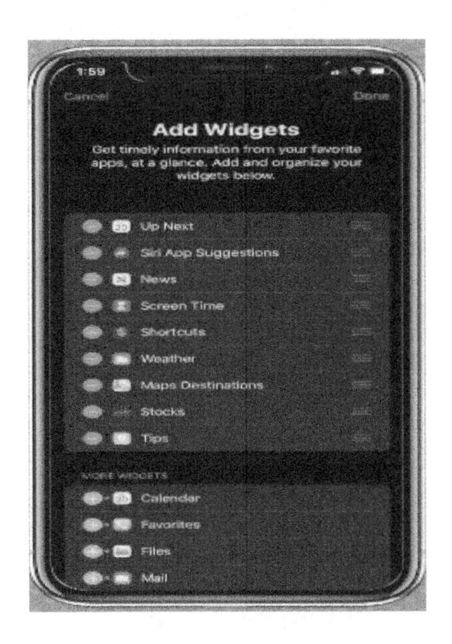

Swipe Typing

Another addition to iOS 13 is the swipe typing feature in your device's default keyboard. This feature allows you to type a word by swiping your finger across the keys of your keyboard rather than tapping on each word. The keyboard then sorts out the rest by deducing the right words you were typing and then inserting it into your message. Although it may take some time for you to get used to it, seeing that it is a new development, however, once you get the hang of it, you will notice that it is faster than tapping each key.

Swipe typing is enabled with iOS 13 and so, you will not need to take any action to turn it on. For instance, say you want to type "call," all you need to do is to tap on the "c" key with your keyboard then swipe your fingers over the "a", "l" and "l" keys in this order. The keyboard will automatically predict the words you wish to type. Once done swiping, the keyboard will present three options for the words you swiped and you click to choose the right one. If the prediction in the center is correct, start swiping your next words to get the keyboard to adopt the last words automatically. The longer you use the keyword the more accurate the predictions become, but when using uncommon words, you may likely have to tap-type first. You can always alternate between swiping and typing whenever you want to without changing any settings.

Disable Swipe Typing

While the swipe typing is enabled by default, you can disable it if you do not find it useful or easy.

- Go to the settings app.
- Click on **General.**
- Then select **Keyboards.**
- Navigate to **"Slide to Type"** and move the switch to the left to disable the option.

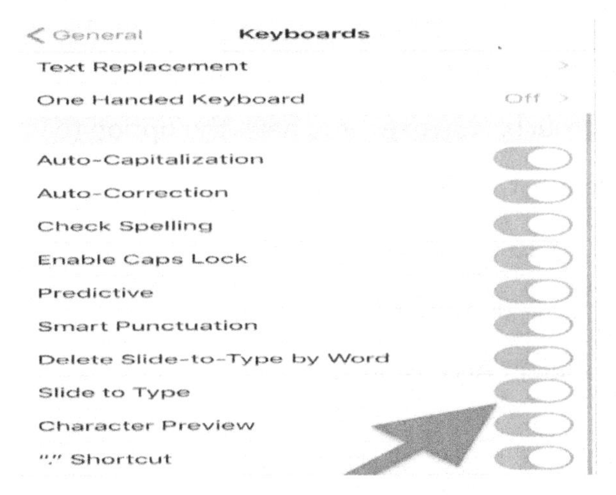

Another way to do this is by using the keyboard itself.

- Long press on the keyboard switcher.
- Then click on **Keyboard settings.**

- Depending on your keyboard setup, you will see the switcher as a Globe icon or an Emoji icon.
- Navigate to **"Slide to Type"** and move the switch to the left to disable the option.

Note: If you have only one keyboard activated on your device, you will be unable to use this option.

Haptic Touch

The iPhone 11 replaced the 3D Touch with the Haptic touch. However, you have the option to disable it with the steps below:

- Go to the settings app.
- Click on **General.**
- Select **Accessibility.**

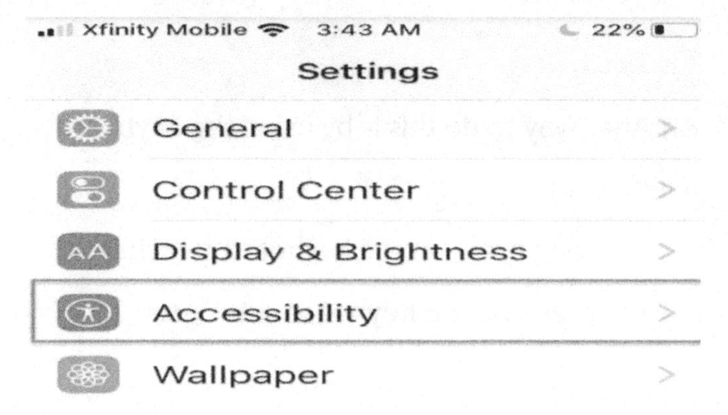

- Then click on **3D and Haptic Touch.**
- Move the switch to the left to disable **3D Touch.**

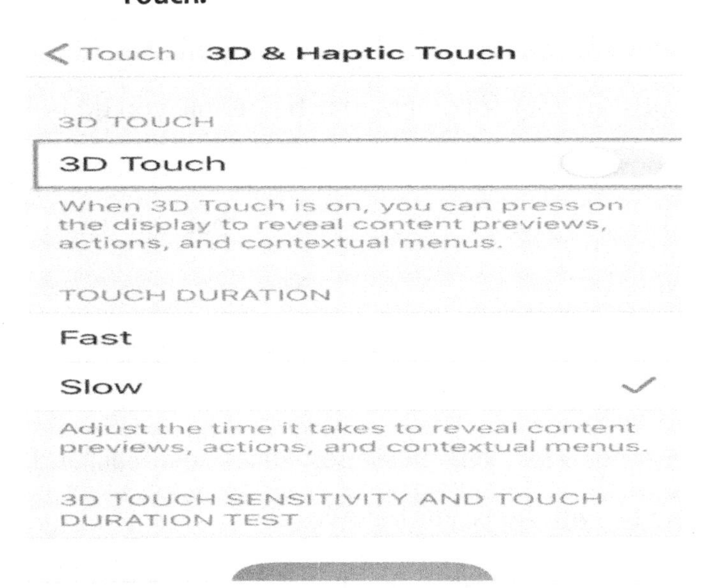

Go through the steps to enable the option whenever you wish to

Remove Location Details from Photos

When you take pictures with your iPhone, the GPS records the exact place you took the photo. This can be beneficial as you can view your photos based on location or occasion. This also means that whenever you share these photos, viewers can find out where you took the photo through their photo app. This may be an issue when posting pictures to social media where most of your followers may be people you do not know personally, and for security reasons, you may not want to post a picture that can lead to your home.

You can remove a location from your videos, photos, movies, or multiple images that you intend to send via messages, Facebook, Mail, and so on with the steps below:

- Capture your pictures in the usual way with your camera app.
- Navigate to the gallery for the photo.
- If sharing a single video or photo, click on it to open, then click on the **Share** button.
- If sharing several videos and photos, click on **Select** in the section view, then click on all the items you wish to share and then click on the **Share** button.

- On the next screen to share, you will notice a button for **Options.**
- Click on **Options** and disable the **Location** on the next screen.
- Then choose your sharing method.

Note: You will have to set this feature each time you want to share a video or picture. The Location details can only be disabled from the iPhones photo app, so you must always share your contents from the app directly. The photos and videos on your phone will continue to have the location details as the feature only affects contents shared with third-party.

Profile Picture and Name in iMessages

With this feature, you can now set a screen name and a profile image on your iMessage that you will share with your selected contacts. So, when next you text another iPhone user, they will not need to save your contact details before they can know who is texting them. Follow the easy steps below to set it up.

- Open the Message app.
- Click on the three dots (...) at the right upper corner of your screen.
- Then click on **Edit Name and Photo.**
- On the next screen, you can choose a profile picture and also input your desired last and first name.
- You can choose to use your personal Memoji as your profile picture or choose from available Animoji.
- Then, choose your preference from the sharing options on the screen: with *Anyone*, *Contacts Only*, or to *Always Ask* if the details are to be shared.

Create and Use Animoji or Memoji

The steps below will show you how to create a Memoji

- Go to name and profile picture settings.

- Click on the circle for pictures close to the name field.
- Then click on the "+" sign to make your own Memoji.

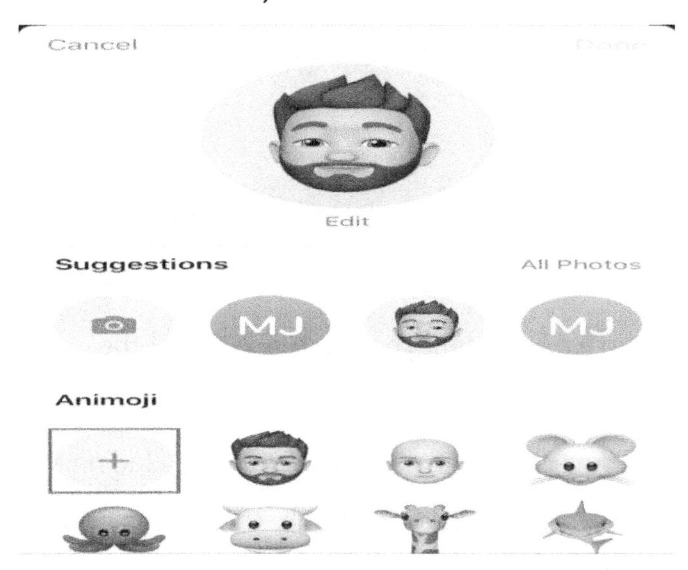

- After you must have created one, click on it to choose a pose for your Memoji and to also use it as your profile picture.

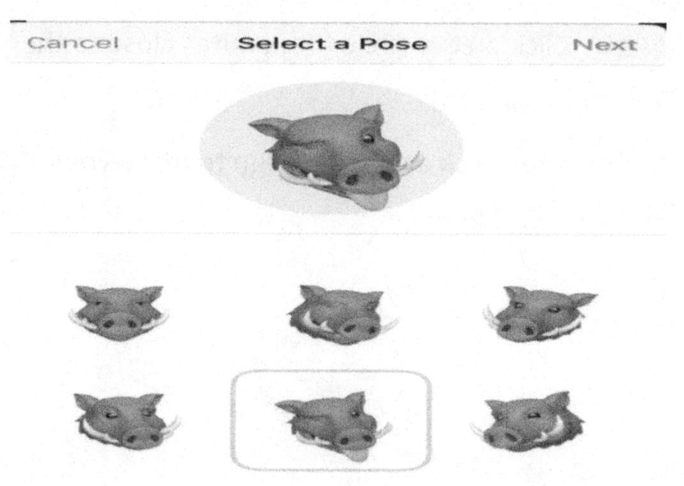

If you rather use something else other than a picture of yourself, you can make use of the Animoji. In the Animoji menu selection, you will find several options to choose from, including a shark, mouse and even a skull. Then pick a pose just like you did with the Memoji. After selecting an Animoji or Memoji, you have to scale it, place it to fit the circle then select a background color to finish the setup.

Profile Picture and Name View in iMessages

It is quite refreshing to have your profile picture and name show especially when messaging a friend; however, you may not want an unknown person to have access to your real names or profile picture. Thankfully, there is a setting to limit who has access to what.

- Go to the settings for **Share Automatically,** then select from the three options available for sharing your name and profile picture.
- Go for **Contacts Only** if you want to share the picture and details with only people in your contact list.
- The **Anyone** option means that everyone and anyone can access this information
- **Always Ask** will give you the option to choose people to share with personally. Each time you receive a message on your phone and you open it, you will receive a small pop-up at the top of your screen asking if you will like to share your details with the sender. Click on **Share** to send

your details across or click on **"X"** to refuse and shut down the message.

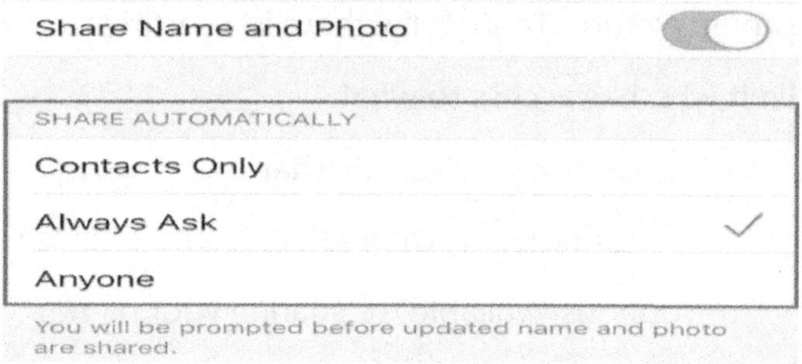

Share Name and Photo

SHARE AUTOMATICALLY

Contacts Only

Always Ask

Anyone

You will be prompted before updated name and photo are shared.

Dark Mode

You wake up in the morning, eager to see your missed notifications, you pick your phone and get almost blinded by the bright white theme of your phone. Thankfully, iOS 13 comes with a new dark mode that can save you from this brightness by changing the white areas in your phone to a much darker tone. This change will apply to all the system apps including Safari and iMessage while Apple has encouraged all third-party developers to add themes that are compatible with the dark mode in their apps. Follow the steps below to find Dark Mode.

- Go to the settings app
- Click on **Display and Brightness**

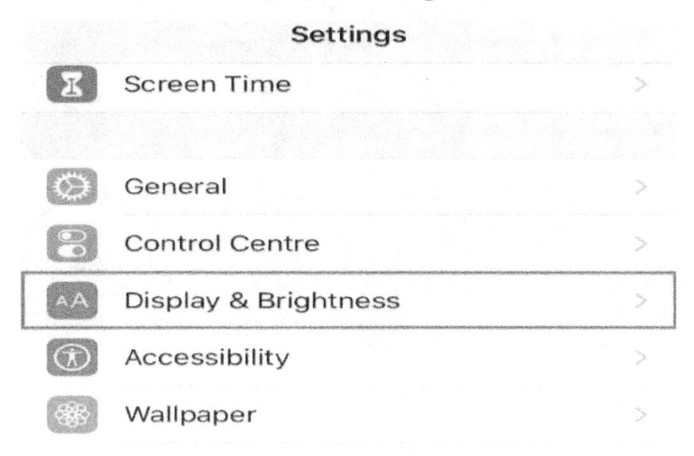

- Then tap on the tick box beneath the Light or Dark themes to activate your preferred one.

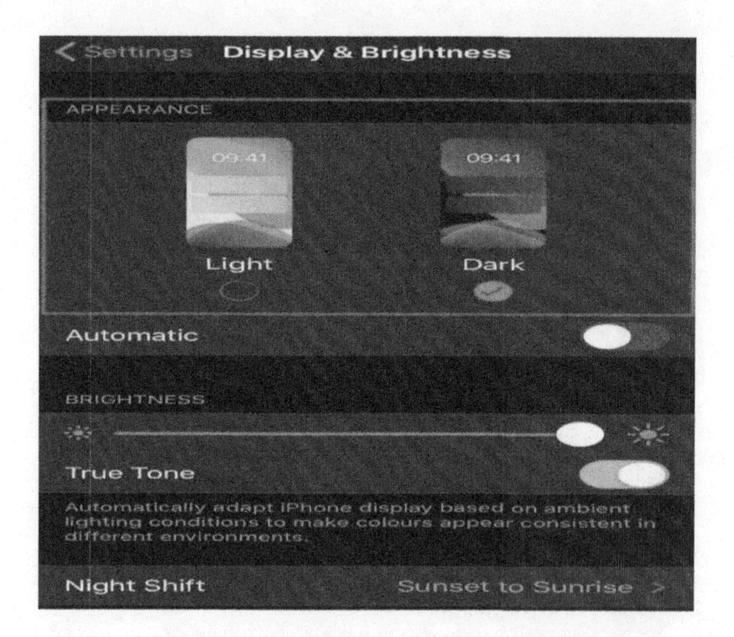

- If you want to set your phone to have a bright theme in the day and a dark theme at night, just hit the toggle for the **Automatic** option and tap the **Options** button under **Automatic** to set when the darker theme should set in.
- Select either **Sunset to Sunrise** option or set to **Custom Schedule.**

< Back Appearance Schedule

Automatically transition iPhone appearance between light and dark based on time preference.

Sunset to Sunrise

Custom Schedule ✓

Light Appearance 07:00

Dark Appearance 22:00

Automatically Activate the Dark Mode

If you wish to use a brighter theme during the day and a darker theme at night, you can do this without having to always go to settings every time to configure. You can configure your settings to interchange the two options at the set time. You can do this with the simple steps below:

- Go to the settings app
- Then click on **Display and Brightness**
- Beside the **Automatic** menu, move the switch to the right to enable it.

- The menu will, by default, change to **Sunset to Sunrise.**
- To edit this, click on **Options** under the **Automatic** menu.
- **Sunset to Sunrise** means that Dark Mode will be activated once the sun goes down using your GPS location.
- You can select ***Custom Schedule*** and input your own desired time for the Dark Mode to kick in.

Set Your Wallpaper to React to Dark Mode

Do you know that some wallpapers in the iPhone 11 can react to the Dark Mode? To set a wallpaper that has a dynamic color-changing feature, follow the simple steps below:

- Go to the settings app.
- Click on **Wallpapers.**
- Select ***Choose a New Wallpaper.***
- Then chose **Stills.**

- Wallpapers that can react when the Dark Mode is enabled have a small circle mark at the right of your screen towards the bottom. You will see a line in the middle of each image displaying what your screen will be like if activated.

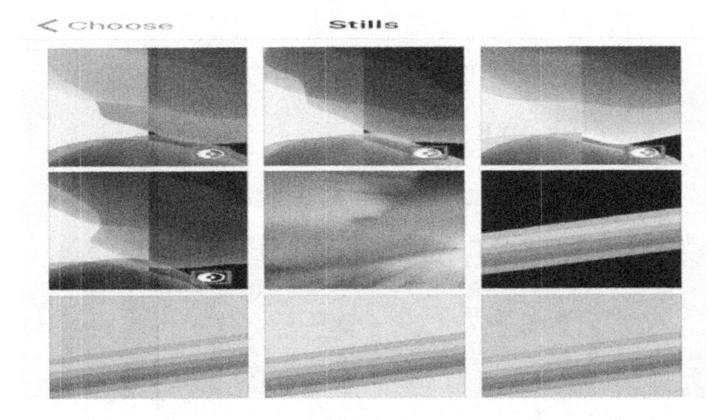

- If you prefer to use your customized wallpaper, return to the **Wallpaper menu**
- Navigate to ***Dark Appearance Dims Wallpaper*** and toggle the switch to the right to enable.
- Although the wallpapers will not react like the reacting ones, however, it will dim a little when the Dark mode is enabled, so

that you don't get dazzled by the lighter areas.

Optimized Battery Charging

You can optimize your battery charging to enable it last longer with the steps below:

- Launch the Settings app.
- Click on **Battery.**
- Navigate to **Battery Health.**

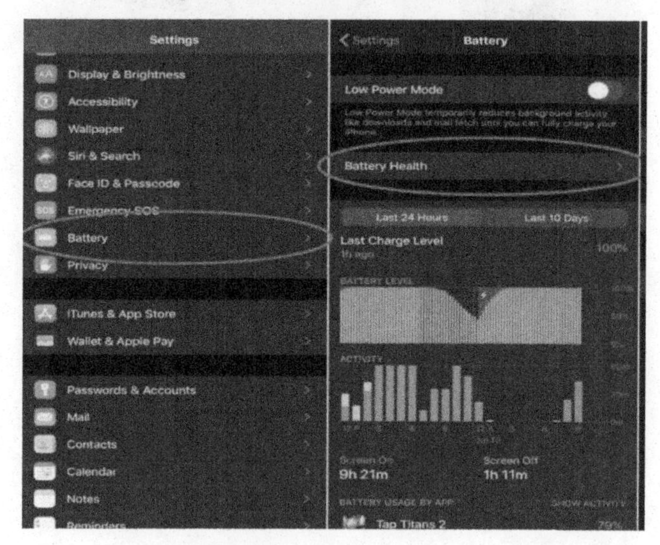

- Under **Battery Health,** you will find the maximum battery capacity left for your battery, an indication of the level of degradation, as well as the option to enable **Optimized Battery Charging.**

- Move the switch beside **Optimized Battery Charging** to the right to enable the feature.

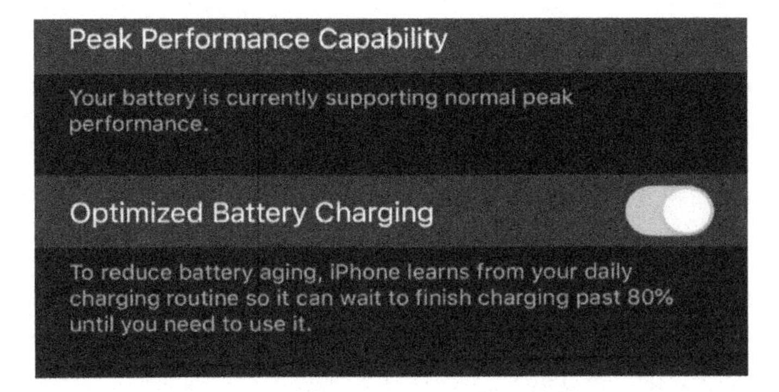

Note: while this feature is on, you may notice that your iPhone could stop charging at 80%. You should not worry as Apple has ensured that the device does not drain battery quick.

iPhone Battery Life Tips

Several things work together to reduce the life of your battery, like plugging the device even after it is fully charged. Below I will list tips that will help to prolong the life of the battery.

- It is important not to let your battery get drained totally. Best is always to keep it at 20 percent and above.
- Avoid exposing the device to excessive heat. It is a terrible idea to charge your iPhone in a scorching environment.
- Quick change from very hot to icy conditions is also terrible for the health of your battery.
- If you intend not to use your phone for a week and above, you should run down the battery to below 80% but not less than 30 percent. Then shut down the phone completely.
- Do not always fully charge your device if not using it for a long time.

Pair your iPhone with a DualShock 4

You can play games on your phone using the DualShock 4 for a better experience. Follow the steps below to pair both devices.

- Go to the settings app.
- Click on **Bluetooth** to enable it.
- With the Bluetooth enabled, ensure that the DualShock 4 controller is well charged.
- Press both the share button and the PlayStation button at the same time and hold down for some seconds.
- Then, you will see the light at the back of the controller begin to flash intermittently.
- Under the Bluetooth menu on your iPhone, you will see DualShock 4 Wireless controller come up as one of the devices.
- Click on it.
- The blinking light at the back of the controller should change to reddish-pink color as an indicator that the devices are paired.

Disconnect a DualShock 4 from your iPhone

When you finish with the game, ensure to turn off the Bluetooth connection. To disconnect through the controller, hold down the PlayStation button for approximately 10 seconds. To disconnect through your iPhone, the best method will be to go through the Control Center with the steps below:

- Use your finger to swipe from the bottom up.
- Hold down the Bluetooth icon on your screen.
- A menu will pop up on your screen, hold down the icon for *Bluetooth: On.*
- Another pop up will show on the screen displaying "DUALSHOCK 4 Wireless Controller" in the list.
- Click on it to disconnect your controller.

Another method you can use is below

- Go to the settings app and click on **Bluetooth.**

- A pop-up will appear on your screen, hold down the icon for *Bluetooth: On.*
- Another pop up will show on the screen displaying "DUALSHOCK 4 Wireless Controller" in the list.
- Click on it to disconnect your controller.

And again, another method can be found below

- Go to the settings app and click on **Bluetooth.**
- On the next screen, under the **My Devices** list, you will find "DUALSHOCK 4 Wireless Controller."
- At the right of this option, you will find an icon with "**i**" in a blue circle. Click on this icon.
- A menu will pop up, then select **Disconnect**.

When next you want to use the controller, press the PlayStation button to connect immediately.

Unpair the DualShock 4 from your iPhone

Usually, the PlayStation may connect by accident when stuffed in your bag, especially when on a trip. In such cases, it is advised to unpair first and then re-pair when you want to use it.

To unpair this device, follow the steps highlighted above to disconnect, but rather than clicking on **Disconnect,** you should click on **"Forget This Device."**

Pair your iPhone with an Xbox One S controller

- Go to the settings app.
- Click on **Bluetooth** to enable it.
- With the Bluetooth enabled, ensure that the **Xbox One controller** is well charged.
- Press the Xbox logo button to turn on the Xbox.
- You will see a wireless enrollment button located at the back of the controller. Press the button and hold it for some seconds.

- If the controller has been unpaired already from a different device, please skip this step as you can just press and hold the Xbox button to put it in pairing mode.
- Then you will see the light of the Xbox button begin to flash quickly.
- Under the Bluetooth menu on your iPhone, you will see the "Xbox Wireless Controller" come up as one of the devices.
- Click on it.
- Once it pairs correctly, the blinking light will stop and remain focused.

Disconnect Xbox One Controller from your iPhone

When done with the game, it is advisable to turn off the Bluetooth connection. To disconnect through the controller, just hold down the Xbox button for approximately 10 seconds.

To disconnect from your iPhone, the best method will be to go through the Control Center with the steps below

- Use your finger to swipe from the bottom up.
- Hold down the Bluetooth icon on your screen.
- A menu will pop up on your screen, hold down the icon for ***Bluetooth: On.***
- Another pop up will show on the screen displaying the **"Xbox Wireless Controller"** on the list.
- Click on it to disconnect your controller.

And another method can be found below

- Go to the settings app and click on **Bluetooth.**
- On the next screen, under the **My Devices** list, you will find the "Xbox Wireless Controller."

- At the right of this option, you will find an icon with "I" in a blue circle. Click on this icon.
- A menu will pop up, then select **Disconnect.**

To use this device again, simply press the Xbox button to get it working.

Copy, Cut, Paste, Redo and Undo Gestures

For most users, the iPhone has become the major way we communicate with people online as well as carry out other document functions.

This is why it is important to have a good text management feature other than the "shake to undo" gesture in the old iOS.

With iOS 13, Apple introduced the three-finger gesture to make it easy for typing. Once you get used to these features, you will enjoy communicating on your iPhone.

Redo and Undo

The **shake to undo** gesture is still available, but the three-finger swipe gesture is sure to override it as users get used to the new addition.

- To undo, swipe to the left with your three fingers on the screen.
- To Redo, swipe to the right with your three fingers on the screen.
- Another way to undo is by double-clicking on the screen with your three fingers.
- If you look at the top of your screen, you will see the badges for "Redo" or "Undo" to verify your action.

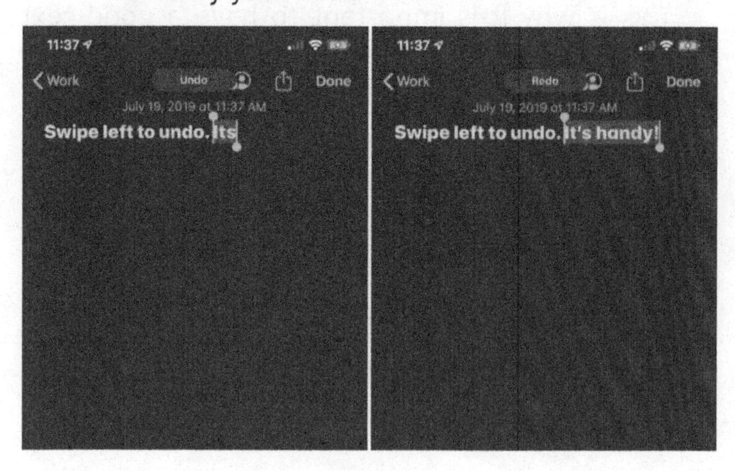

Copy, Cut and Paste

To best perform this feature, I will advise you to use your two fingers and your thumb.

- To copy, use your three fingers to pinch on the text and then un-pinch (expand) using your three fingers to Paste the copied text.
- Perform the copy gesture twice with your finger to cut out the text. While the first gesture will copy the text, repeating it the second time will cut out the text.
- If you look at the top of your screen, you will see the badges for "Copy," "Cut," or "Paste" to verify your action.

Cursor Movement on iPhone 11

The way the cursor moves has also changed with iOS 13 and iPhone 11. To drag around a text entry, simply click on the entry cursor.

You no longer have to wait for some time before picking up text, once you touch it, you can move it immediately to where you want to place it. Sadly, the little magnifying glass that pops up on the screen is no more, and this can make it a little difficult to make a precise cursor placement as you will be unable to see the characters that you have picked.

Shortcut Bar

If you think that the gestures are difficult to use, then you can make use of the new shortcut bar. On any part of the screen, including the keyboard area, click and hold on the screen with your three fingers for approximately a second to launch the shortcut bar. The bar will appear above the screen with buttons for **Cut, Undo, Copy, Redo, and Paste.** You will continue to see the bar as you repeat the command, and then it disappears as soon as you enter text or move the cursor.

New Volume Indicator

The new volume indicator introduced in iOS 13 is less obtrusive, and you can now pull it down and up. Several users have complained of the giant volume indicator for years, and Apple finally used a small vertical bar placed at the top left of the screen to replace it. Use your finger to drag the bar down and up. When you do this, an indicator will show at the end of the volume bar showing the output of your device sound, for example, Bluetooth device Airpods or speaker.

Download Large Apps over Cellular Network

You no longer have to wait for Wi-fi connection to be able to download large apps. Before now, your iOS will always warn you to connect to wi-fi to download large files, but with iOS 13, when downloading apps over 200MB, you will receive a pop-up on your screen asking if you want to download with cellular or if you will wait for Wi-fi.

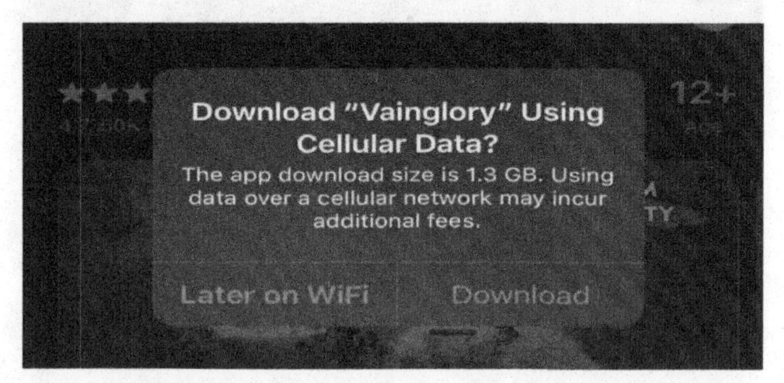

- Go to the settings app.
- Click on the **iTunes & App Store.**
- Here, you can set the iOS always to allow you download your apps over cellular or always ask you if you want to continue or ask you only when the app is over 200MB.

Scan Documents Straight to Files App

The new inbuilt scanner allows you to scan your documents, save as PDFs, and even choose your preferred folder for storage. You can now scan a document to PDF and also save it automatically in Files. To use this feature, follow the steps below.

- Go to the Files app.
- From any location in the app, pull down a little to display the options for the View (View and Sorting style).
- Click on the 3-dot (...) icon at the left side of your screen, there, you will see the option to **scan a document, create a new folder, or connect to a server**.

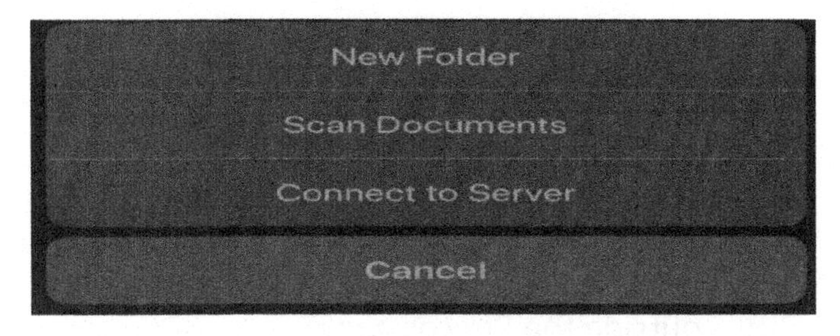

- Scan your receipts or forms as a PDF and get it saved in the cloud folder of your choice.

Save Screenshots to the Files App

You can save all your screenshots in your Files app rather than the photos app with the steps below:

- Take your screenshot then click on the little preview in the Markup to edit it.
- Click on **Done.**
- You will see a new option on your screen. Added to the **Delete Screenshot** and **Save to Photos** options is the option to **Save to Files.**
- The **Save to Files** option allows you to save the screenshots in your network folders or iCloud or other Files location outside the Photos app.

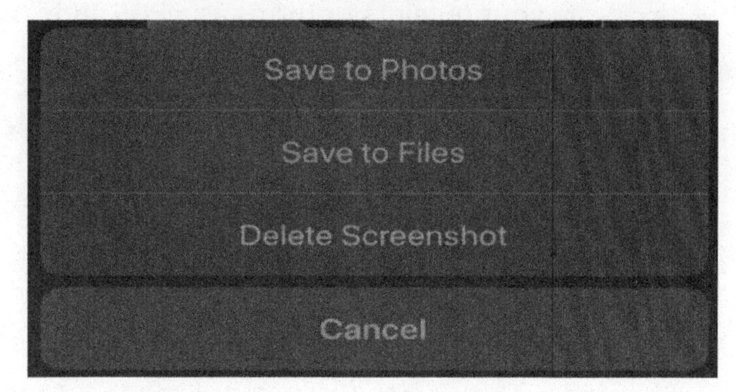

Zoom Voice Memos

If you use voice memos a lot, you may have always wanted to have more control over editing or trimming your voice memos. To do this,

- Go to your voice memo
- Click on **Edit,** and then you can pinch on the screen to zoom the waveform. This will give you better control, and also make it easy for you to scrub through recordings that are very long.

Voice Control

The voice control feature allows you to control your phone using your voice more than Siri can do. For instance, you can say "Launch Instagram" Or "open YouTube" without touching your phone, and your iPhone will immediately carry out your command. The steps below will show you how to set up this feature.

- Go to the settings app.
- Click on **Accessibility.**

- Then select **Voice Control.**
- Follow the instructions on your screen to complete the setup.
- To know that voice control is active, you will see a blue microphone icon at the left top side of your screen, close to the clock.

Note: whenever the voice control is enabled, it always listens for your command, and so, it may not be safe to use in public to avoid your phone from being snatched or stolen.

Delete Apps

You can now delete apps from your device with the steps below:

- long press on the desired app in your home screen to display an action to rearrange apps.
- Click on this option to get all the apps to wiggle while you will see an **X mark** beside each icon.

- Tap on the **X** beside the apps you wish to remove.

You can also delete apps from the App store. When viewing apps from the app store or updating apps, swipe to the left on any app you want to delete from the list, to give you the option to **Delete.** This makes it convenient to remove any app you no longer need from your app store without having to exit the store. Let me explain the steps in details

- Go to the App Store on your device.
- Click on your account picture located at the right top corner of your screen.
- Navigate to the section for **Updated Recently.**
- To delete any app that was updated recently, swipe to the left on the desired app in the list.
- Then click the red button that you see on your screen.

Delete Apps from the Update Screen

Although the usual way is still active, there is another way to save time.

- Go to the app store. You will see that the updates for the app are now in your **account card.** (click on your picture at the right top of your screen)
- If there are any apps on that list, you want to delete, pull the app to your left, and an option will come up to delete the app.
- This applies to all the apps on the list, whether it has a pending update or not.

How to Enable Automatic Software Updates

Sometimes we get carried away with our busy schedules and forget to update our phone software to the latest version. Thankfully, there is a way to set your device to update once there are new versions automatically.

- Go to the settings app.

- Click on **General**
- Then select **Software Update.**
- Navigate to **Automatic Updates** and move the switch to the right to enable the feature.

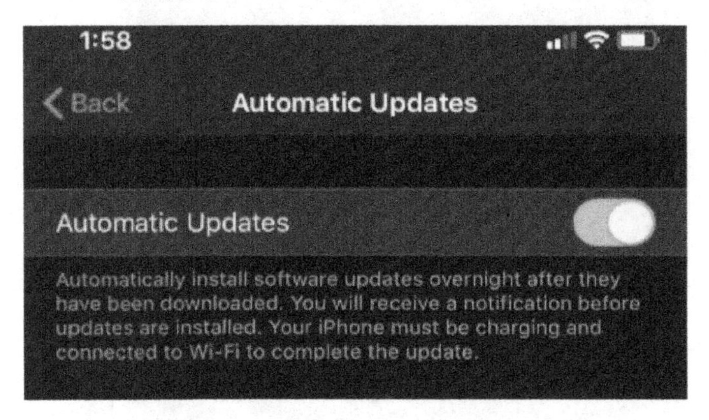

Modify video Quality

You can capture 4k resolution videos with your new iPhone at 60 frames per second. Follow the steps below to modify the video settings

- Go to the settings app.
- Click on **Camera** then click on **Record Video.**
- On the next screen, you will get various options, including 4K at 60 FPS. You will

also see an estimate of the storage for a minute video for each of the settings.

- Select the **4K at 60 FPS** option to use this feature.

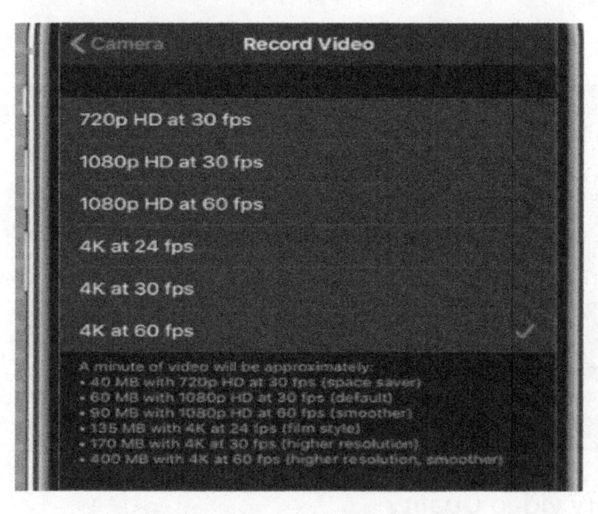

Record 4K Video from Selfie Camera

- Go to the camera app.
- Click on **Camera.**
- Then click on **Record Video**
- Then set the front-facing camera to 4K.

Edit Photos and Rotate Videos

Other iOS lacked its editing tools until iOS 13. Now, you can go to your Photo app to modify various vital parts of your videos and photos. To do this,

- Go to your Photos app.
- Choose your desired photo and then click on the **Edit** button.
- On the next screen, you can try to swipe between options and adjust sliders to see how your picture will look when modified with several options
- You can also do this for the videos.

Apply Filter to a Video

To apply a filter, similar to the ones used on Instagram, to videos that you have captured already, follow the instructions below.

- Open the photo apps on your device.
- Choose a video from the photo library.

- Click on **Edit** at the right top side of your screen.

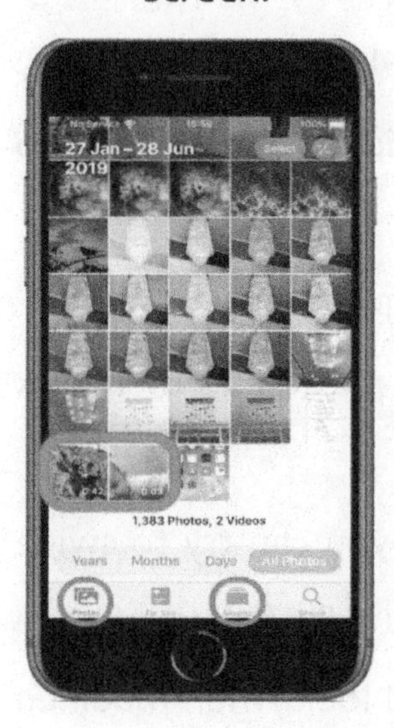

- Click on the Filter menu located at the end of your screen (it has a shape like a Venn diagram)

- Move through the available nine filters to see how each will look on your video.
- Select your preferred filter, and you will see a horizontal dial under the filter you selected.
- With your finger, slide the dial to adjust the level of intensity of that filter.
- Click on **Done** at the right bottom side of your screen to effect the filter on your video.

Switch to Ultra-Wide Camera

To quickly switch to the ultra-wide camera while using the camera app, click on the 0.5x button on the camera view.

Burst Mode Photos

Click on the shutter button and then swipe left to capture photos in burst mode.

Filter Intensity

When you click on a photo to edit it, you can set the filter intensity once you have selected a new filter.

Lighting Mode Photo Effects

When you capture a picture while in portrait mode, the device makes use of the dual camera to create a depth-of-the-field effect, which will allow you to create a photo that has a blurred background with a sharp subject. The iPhone 11 has another feature called the High-Key Light Mono. This is similar to the white and black effect of the Stage Light Mono. However, you get only a white background without the black effect.

- Go to the Photo app on your device.
- Click on a portrait photo from your library to select it.
- Confirm that the image was captured in a portrait mode by checking for the portrait label, usually at the left top corner of your screen.

- Then click on **Edit** at the right top corner to go into an editing mode.

- Select the portrait icon in the tools bar at the bottom row, then choose a lighting mode by sliding along the icons under the photos with your finger.
- After you have selected a lighting mode like the High-Key Light Mono effect, a slider will appear below it.
- Move the slider to rachet up or dial down the lighting effect intensity.
- Click on **Done** once you are satisfied with how the image looks.

Block Spam Calls

With this feature, you can stop all spam calls from ringing on your phone without blocking each number separately. So, every spam call will go straight to voicemail. This way, if you find out that the number is not spam, you can just go to your voicemails to check for the call, and call back anyone that you need to contact. Follow the steps highlighted below to activate the new call blocker:

- Go to your settings app.
- Click on **Phone.**
- Then move the switch beside ***Silence Unknown Callers*** to the right to enable it.

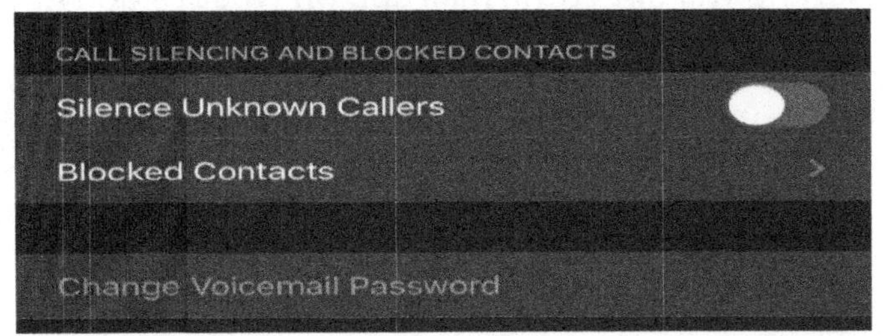

Once this feature is active, unknown callers will be sent straight to voicemail by default, and you won't have to worry about robocalls, spam calls, and other distractions.

Block Spam, Contacts and Unknown Senders in Mail App

This feature will set the incoming emails from blocked senders to go directly to the trash folder. You are not really blocking the senders as you can always view their messages in the trash folder. This option is better than totally blocking the contact. Currently, Apple has grouped all spammers and contacts that are blocked into a single folder.

The first step is to select your block settings. This setting will direct the mail app on what to do with the blocked contacts.

- Go to the settings app.
- Click on **Mail.**
- Then navigate to **Threading.**
- Click on **Blocked Sender,** and you will see three options

- If you choose **None,** it will disable email blocking.
- **"Mark as Blocked, Leave in Inbox"** means that the emails will come to your inbox, but you will not receive notifications like the other emails.
- **Move to Trash,** will move emails from blocked contacts to your trash folder. You can then set to empty the folder or have it deleted automatically, manually.

Note: this feature will apply to all the accounts you have in your mail app, including Outlook, Gmail, Yahoo, etc.

Block a Sender from Received Emails

When you receive an email from someone you do not know or do not want to hear from again, you can block the person straight from the email.

- Click on the contact fields at the top of the email to show you all the parties on the send list.
- Then click on the email address you want to block.
- The next screen will show you an expanded menu option.
- Click on **Block this contact.**
- Click on it again in the prompt to confirm your action.
- The contact is blocked!
- All emails from the sender, whether present or past, will have a blocked hand icon close to the date in the header for email. You will also see a notification at the top of the email reading, **"This**

message is from a sender in your blocked list."

Unblock a Sender from Received Email

If you change your mind about a sender, simply go back to the sender's contact details in the email and click on "Unblock this Contact." It may take some seconds for the hand icon to disappear, but the sender will be unblocked instantly.

Block a Contact from Settings

In case you do not have any email from the person you want to block, you can go to settings to stop them from sending any more messages.

- From the settings app, click on **Mail.**
- Then scroll down and click on **Blocked.**
- You will see all the email addresses and phone numbers that you have ever blocked on this screen.

- At the bottom of your screen, click on **"Add New."**
- Then select the contacts you want to block once prompted.
- You will then see the numbers and email addresses in the blocked list.

Note: This option only works with saved contacts.

Unblock a Contact from Settings

You can unblock all categories of blocked people from your settings since every single contact or sender blocked appears on the settings menu. To do this,

- follow the steps above to access the list of your blocked contacts.
- Then short-swipe from the left on the email address or phone number you want to unblock.
- Click on **Unblock.**

- Another way is to long swipe on the contact to automatically unblock it.
- Or you can click on **Edit** at the right top of your screen, click on the red "-" minus button beside the email address or phone number you want to unblock, then click on **Unblock.**

Dialing from the Phone App

- Tap the Phone icon on the left.
- Click on Keypads to show the keypads.
- Input the number you want to call then press the call icon.
- Click on the end call button at the lower part of the screen once done.

Answering Call

- Tap any of the volume keys to silence the call notification when a call comes in.
- If the screen lock is active, slide right to answer the call.

- Click on **Accept**, if there is no screen lock.
- Click on the end call button at the lower part of the screen once done.

Call Waiting

- From **Settings,** click on **Phone** then **Call Waiting.**
- Move the icon beside it to the left or right to enable or disable call waiting.

Call Voicemail

- Click on the phone icon at the left of the home screen.
- Select **'Voicemail'** at the bottom-right corner of the screen.
- Click on **Call Voicemail** in the middle of the screen and listen for instructions.
- Click on the end call button at the lower part of the screen once done.

Call Announcement

Your device can read out the caller's name when there is an incoming call. The number has to be in your address book for this to work.

- From **Settings,** go to **Phone** then **Announce Call.**
- Select **Always** if you want this feature to work when silent mode is off.
- Choose **Headphones & Car** to activate when your device is connected to a car or a headset.
- The **Headphones Only** option will be for when the device is connected to the headset.
- Select **Never** if you do not wish to turn off this feature.

Add Contacts

- At the **Home** screen, select **Extras.**
- Click on **Contacts.**

- Then select the **Add Contact** icon at the right upper side of your screen.
- Enter the details of your contact, including the name, phone number, address, etc.
- Once done inputting the details, tap **Done,** and your new contact has been saved.

Save Your Voicemail Number

- Once you insert your SIM into your new device, it automatically saves your voicemail number.

Merge Similar Contacts

- At the **Home** screen, select **Extras.**
- Click on **Contacts.**
- Click on the contact you want to merge and click on **Edit.**
- At the bottom of the screen, select **Link Contact.**
- Choose the other contact you want to link.
- Click on **Link** at the top right side of the screen.

Copy Contact from Social Media and Email

- From Settings, go to **Accounts and Password.**
- Click on the account, e.g., Gmail.
- Switch on the option beside **Contacts.**

Auto Close Open Tabs in Safari

Launch the Safari browser on your iPhone and click on the **View Tabs.** If you are like me, you probably have several open tabs from search results to opened social media posts and so on. Some you want to close but could be quite tiring to close each individually. Thankfully, iOS added a feature to automatically close open tabs in the Safari after a defined time. Follow the steps to activate

- Go to the settings app.
- Navigate to the Safari setting and click on it.

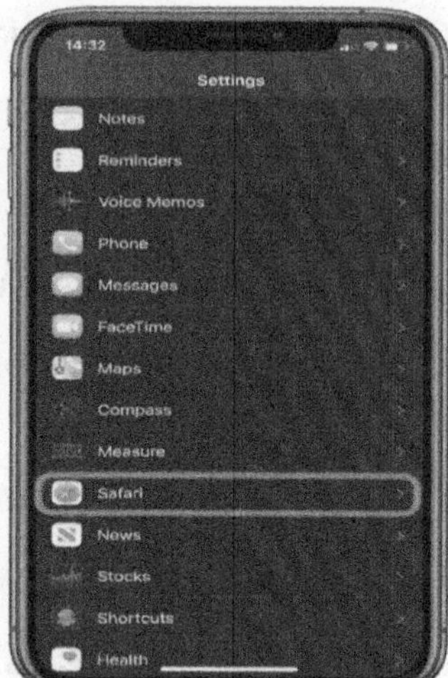

- You will see several options, navigate to the **Tabs** option, then click on **Close Tabs.**
- On the next screen, you will find further options. By default, the selection is set to **Manually.**
- You can set to either **After One Week, After One Day, or After One Month.**

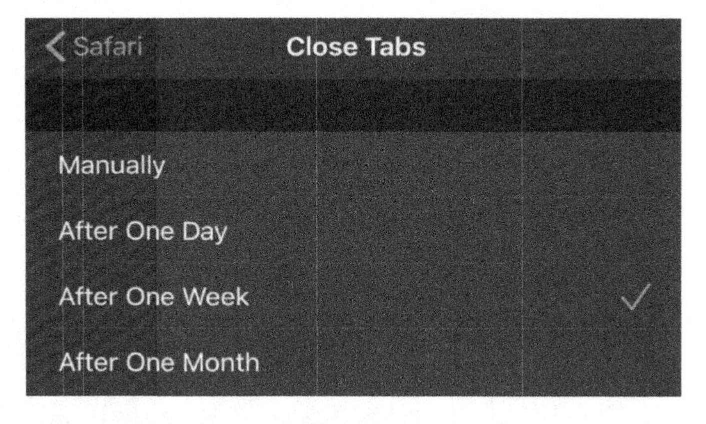

- There is no right or wrong selection. It all depends on your usage, for me, I know that most times I never get to go back to the tabs after a week which is why I selected the "**After one-week**" option.

Safari Website Settings

You can now customize settings for individual sites. Similar to what we have on Safari on Mac, you can modify different security and viewing options for various websites from the website settings. Safari will automatically apply the settings so that you do not have to repeat them. I have highlighted the steps below

- Go to a site that you visit regularly.
- Click on the "aA" icon at the left top corner of your screen to show the **View menu** of the website.
- Then click on **Website settings.**

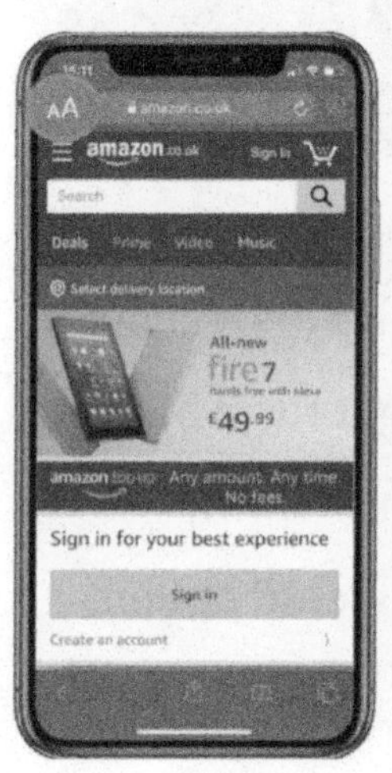

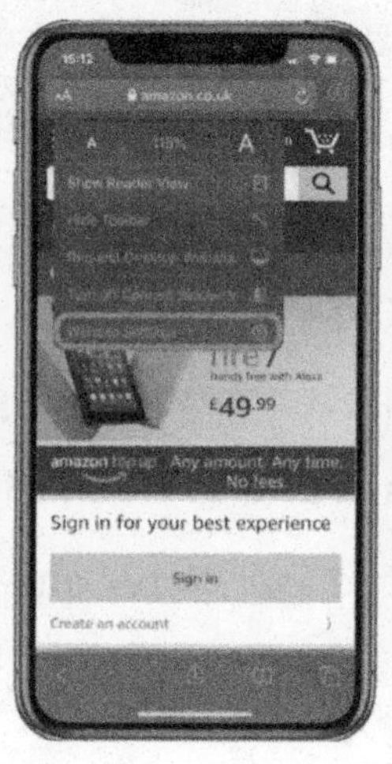

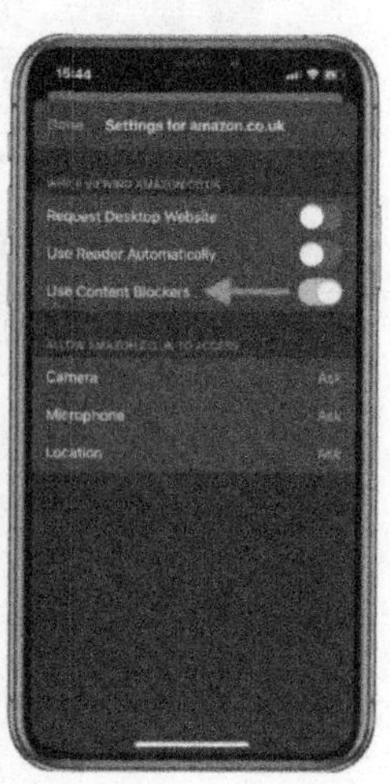

- **Reader Mode** option helps to make online articles more readable by removing extraneous web page contents from it. You can enable this icon by clicking on **"Use Reader Automatically"** to activate this feature by default.

- **Request Desktop Website:** click on this to view original desktop versions of a website on your mobile device.
- **Camera, Microphone, Location:** these last three options allow you to choose if you want sites to have access to your device microphone, camera, as well as your location. You can choose either **Deny** or **Allow,** but if you will rather change your options per time, then you should select the option for **Ask.** This way, whenever sites want to access these features, Safari will first seek your consent.

Auto-Clear Download List in Safari

The upgrade introduced a Download manager in the mobile version of the Safari browser similar to what is obtainable in Windows and Mac. By default, the list clears at the end of each day. However, you can set to remove the list once the download is done or go for the manual way of clearing lists.

- Go to the settings app.
- Click on **Safari.**

- Then click on **Downloads.**
- Click on **Remove Download List Items**.
- Select any of the options on your screen:

  Upon successful download, After one day, or Manually.

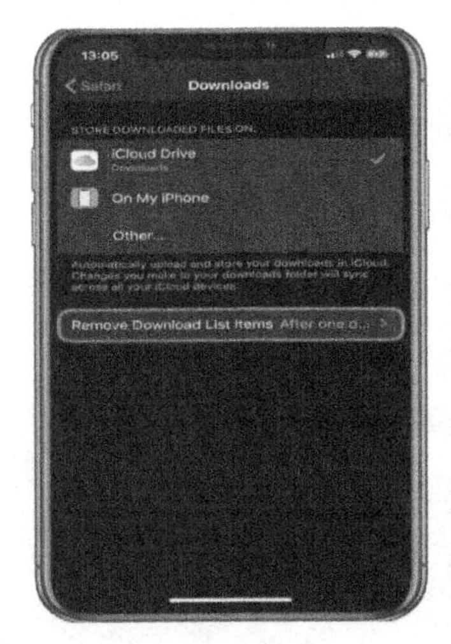

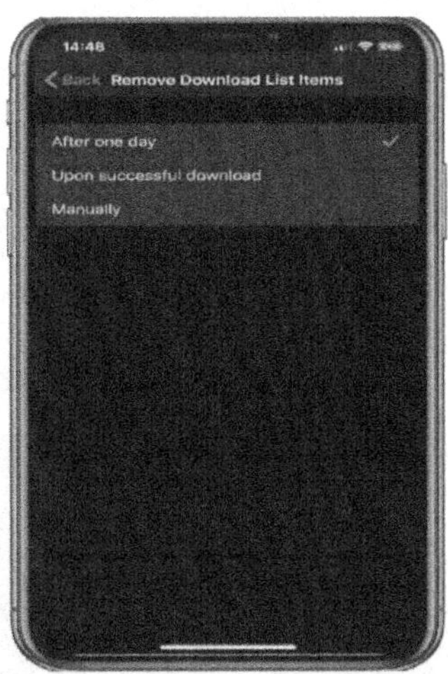

Ad Tracking

The phone automatically brings up ads based on our interest when surfing on Safari. If you do not like to get these interest-based ads when using Safari, you can go to your phone setting to limit ad tracking, that way, you will see less of interest-based adverts when surfing the web.

- Go to the settings app.
- Click on **Privacy.**
- Click on **Advertising** at the bottom of the screen.

- Go to **Limit Ad Tracking** and move the switch to the right to enable this feature.
- The number of ads you receive may not reduce, but they will no longer be displayed based on your interests.

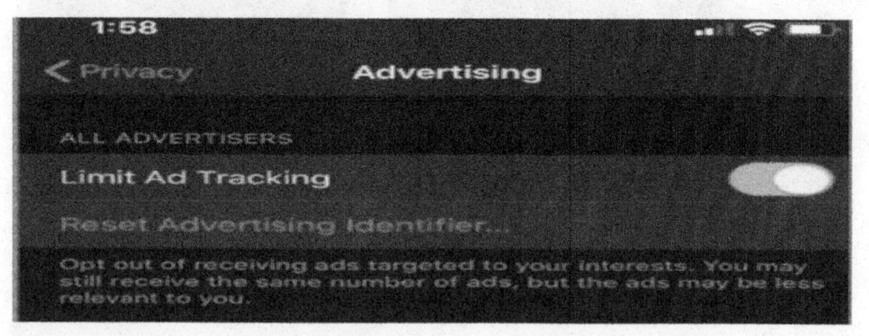

Safari Download Manager

Those who use the Safari desktop version will be more familiar with the Downloads pane in the browser, which informs you of downloaded items, as well as currently downloading items. Now, you can see such with the mobile version of the browser. When you want to download a file, you will see a little download icon at the right top corner of your screen. Click on the icon to see the status of your downloads, click on the magnifying glass close to the downloaded file to go to the folder where the download is located either on the cloud or your iPhone.

Modify Where Downloaded Files from Safari are Saved

By default, all downloaded files are saved in the **Download folder** of the Files app but you can modify this by selecting an alternative storage location with the steps below:

- Go to the settings app.
- Click on **Safari.**
- Then click on **Downloads.**

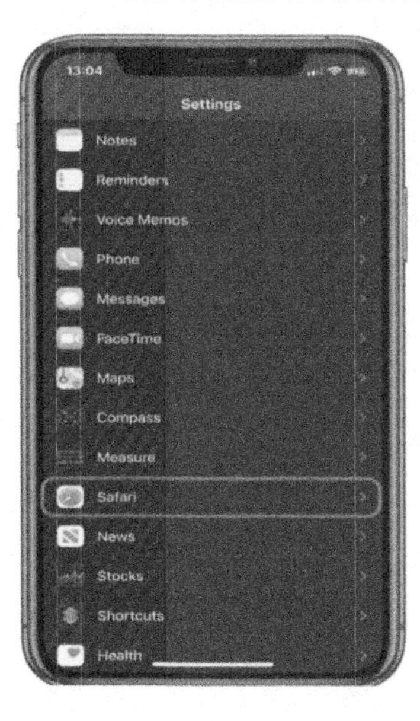

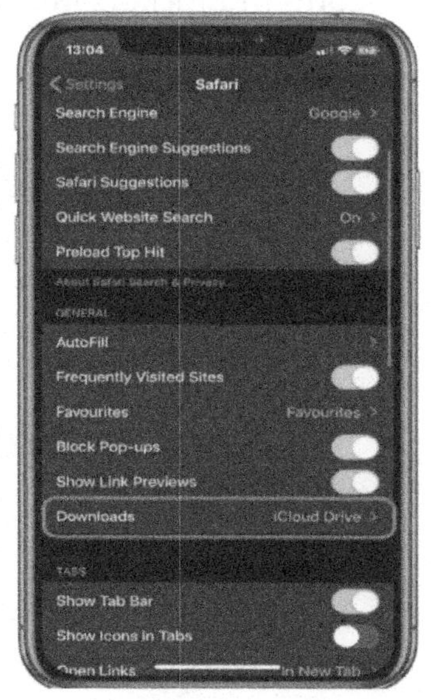

- You can then make your choice from the available options: On My iPhone, iCloud Drive, or in another location that you want.

Content Blockers in Safari

- Go to the settings app.
- Click on **Safari.**

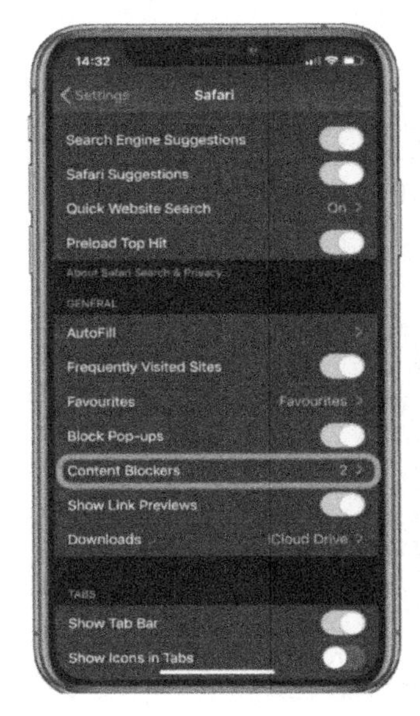

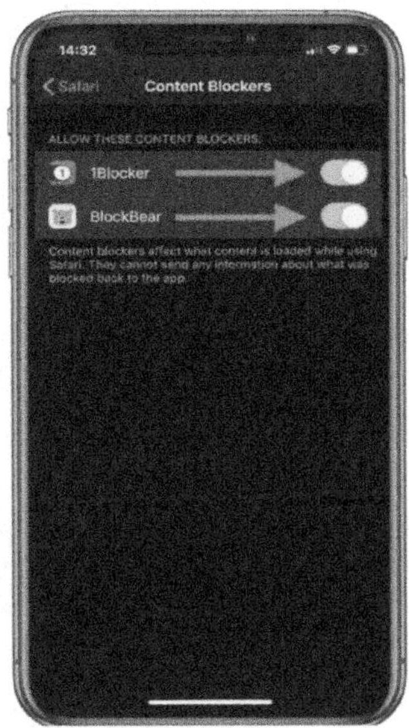

- Go to the **General** option and click on **Content Blockers.**
- Move the switch beside it to the right to enable the option

Note: this option will not be available if you do not install a minimum of one 3rd party content blocker from the store.

Disable Content Blockers Temporarily in Safari

Content blockers help to stop ads like banners and popups from loading on any website you visit. It may also disable beacons, cookies, and others to protect your privacy and prevent the site from tracking you online. Sometimes, the feature may block an element that you need to access, like a web form. If you notice that a useful page element is not coming up because of the content blocker, you can disable it temporarily with the steps below:

- Go to the Safari browser and type in the desired site to visit
- Click on the "aA" icon at the left top corner of your screen to show the View menu of that site.
- Click on" **Turn Off Content Blockers."**

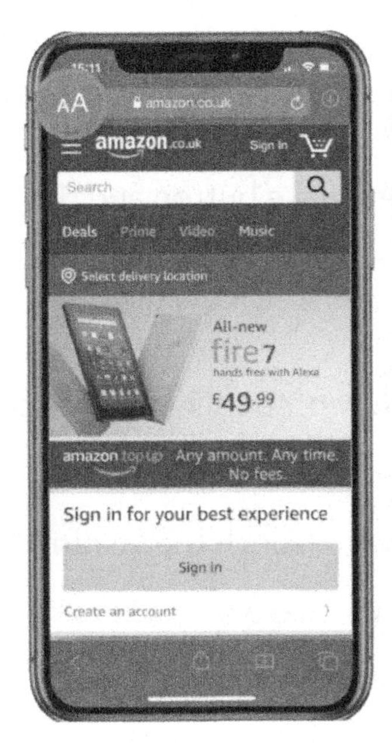

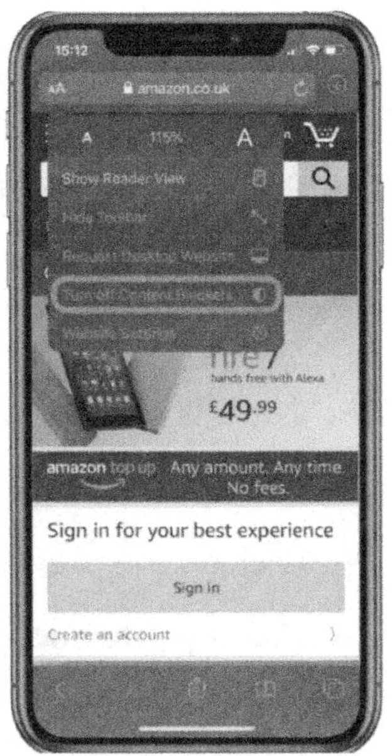

- If you want this disabled for a particular website only, click on **Website Settings,** and then move the switch beside **Use Content Blockers** to the left to disable it.

Share or Save a Safari Web Page as a PDF

This option is only available with the Safari browser. Follow the steps to access this feature.

- Open the Safari app on your device.

- Go to the webpage you want to save as PDF.
- Press both the Sleep/wake button and the Home button at the same time to take a screenshot.
- You will see a preview of the screenshot at the left lower side of the screen.
- Click on the preview to launch the **Instant Markup Interface.** You have only 5 secs before this screen disappears.
- Click on the **Full-Page** option in the right upper corner of the Markup interface.
- Click on **Done,** then select **Save PDF to Files** to save as PDF.
- Click on the **Share** button to share the PDF and choose who and how you want to share it from that screen.

Complete iPhone 11 Reset Guide: How to perform a Soft, Hard, Factory Reset or Master Reset

Most minor issues that occur with the iPhone 11 can be resolved by restarting the device or doing a soft reset. If the soft reset fails to solve the problem, then you can carry out other resets like the hard reset and master reset. Here, you will learn how to use each of the available reset methods.

How to Restart/ Soft Reset iPhone

This is by far the commonest solutions to many problems you may encounter on the iPhone 11. It helps to remove minor glitches that affect apps or iOS as well as gives your device a new start. This option doesn't delete any data from your phone, so you have your contents intact once the phone comes up. You have two ways to restart your device.

Method 1:

- Hold both sides and Volume Down (or Volume Up) at the same time until the slider comes up on the screen.
- Move the slider to the right for the phone to shut down.
- Press the **Side** button until the Apple logo shows on the screen.
- Your iPhone will reboot.

Method 2:

- Go to **Settings** then **General.** Click on **Shut Down.**
- This will automatically shut down the device.
- Wait for some seconds, then Hold the **Side** button to start the phone.

Hard Reset/ Force Restart

There are some cases when you may need to force restart your phone. These are mostly when the screen is frozen and can't be turned off, or the screen is unresponsive. Just like the soft reset, this will not wipe the data on your device. It is important to confirm that the battery isn't the cause of the issue before you begin to force-restart.

Follow the steps below to force-restart:

- Press the **Volume Up** and quickly release.
- Press the **Volume Down** and quickly release.
- Hold down the Side button until the screen goes blank and then release the button and allow the phone to come on.

Factory Reset (Master Reset)

A factory reset will erase every data stored on your iPhone 11 and return the device to its original form from the stores. Every single data from settings to personal data saved on the phone will be deleted. It is important to create a backup before you go through this process. You can either backup to iCloud or iTunes. Once you have successfully backed up your data, please follow the steps below to wipe your phone.

- From the **Home** screen, click on **Settings.**
- Click on **General.**
- Select **Reset**.
- Chose the option to **Erase All Content and Settings.**
- When asked, enter your passcode to proceed.
- Click **Erase iPhone** to approve the action.

Depending on the volume of data on your phone, it may take some time for the factory reset to complete.

Once the reset is done, you may choose to set up with the **iOS Setup Assistant/ Wizard** where you can choose to restore data from a previous iOS or proceed to set the device as a fresh one.

iCloud Troubleshooting

If your iCloud isn't working, use the guide below:

- Ensure the Wi-fi is connected and strong as this is usually the main reason for iCloud backup not to respond.
- Once done, confirm that you have enough space in the cloud. Apple provides only 5G free. If you have used up the space, clear the files you don't need or back them up with iTunes, then remove them from the iCloud backup.
- If you do not wish to delete any information, the next step will be to purchase an additional room in the cloud.
- Lastly, remove any unwanted data from the iPhone or computer before you perform the iCloud backup.

Conclusion

Now that you have all there is to know about your new iPhone 11 and iOS 13, I am confident that you will enjoy operating your device.

All relevant areas concerning the usage of the iPhone 11 from unboxing to the several functions, has been carefully outlined and discussed in detail to make users more familiar with its operations as well as other information not contained elsewhere.

If you are pleased with the content of this book, don't forget to recommend this book to a friend.

Thank you.

Other Books by the Same Author

- Apple TV 4K/ HD User Guide https://amzn.to/2kqpBq4
- Amazon Echo Dot 3rd Generation User Guide https://amzn.to/2kE3X1T
- Kindle Oasis 3 10th Generation User Guide https://amzn.to/2kGM42w
- Mastering your iPhone XR for beginners, seniors, and new iPhone users https://amzn.to/2mgegtc
- Samsung Note 10 and Note 10 Plus User Guide https://amzn.to/2mjBTRG
- Fire TV Stick User Guide https://amzn.to/2kQwTDP
- iPhone 11 Pro Max User Guide https://amzn.to/2lSEBOc
- Beginner's Guide to iPadOS https://amzn.to/2o2w7VJ
- Mastering your iPad 7th gen https://amzn.to/2oAIVmh

Made in the USA
Las Vegas, NV
26 May 2024